# Leadership Profiles from Bible Personalities

Compiled by
Ernest E. Mosley

BROADMAN PRESS
Nashville, Tennessee

4225-32
ISBN: 0-8054-2532-2

Dewey Decimal Classification: 253
Subject headings: MINISTERS // LEADERSHIP

Library of Congress Catalog Card Number: 78-74503
Printed in the United States of America

# Contents

# Introduction

Ernest E. Mosley

Since 1967 I have talked with many pastors who felt that the exacting demands of leadership in pastoral ministry slipped up on them. For some reason they had not equipped themselves through personal or institutional studies with the leadership skills required in volunteer organizations. One pastor of a large church in a college town confessed that he must either find a way to learn better how to lead the employed and volunteer workers in the church or leave the pastorate. He declared that he would not go on until retirement fumbling the ball in leadership. There was no reason to live with the ulcers such a mismatch produced.

Many who have entered the pastoral ministry have done so on the basis of a preaching model. Others were impressed most by the effective pastoral care they received from a pastoral minister. This is particularly true of those who decide during high school or college years that their lives should be spent in pastoral ministry. They have often participated in worship services in which the pastor preached. They have attended weddings and funerals where he nurtured people. The pasto-

7

the neighborhood coffee shop. While the book was written for church leaders, one California businessman found it to be such an effective compilation of leadership information that he obtained a copy for all management personnel in his company.

Now the presses of many publishers are often used in printing materials on leadership for pastoral ministers. Most of these materials provide some ideas that may be of real value to the reader. Most of these draw their insights from the psychological area and relate them to the practice of ministry. Some of them call attention to the evidence of their teachings in the life and work of Jesus and other Bible personalities.

*Leadership Profiles from Bible Personalities* had its birth in the conviction that the Bible should be the primary text for students of leadership. Its strong leaders and its weak leaders—we should be grateful that the record of both is preserved—provide us with valuable lessons. We can see ourselves in leadership situations as we study the experiences of those who were involved in the mission of God in the world. Rather than asking that a passage of Scripture provide us with material for a sermon or Bible lesson, we can ask it to help us understand ourselves and how we can lead others effectively.

As we read the Scriptures in search of leadership learnings, we will discover that the truth has been recorded for centuries. We will be reminded that many of the "new ideas" of contemporary writers were first shared with us in the Bible. Contemporary literature can be studied with greater appreciation as we see the leadership issues discussed against the backdrop of the biblical revelation.

The writers whose works are compiled in this volume have four things in common: a high regard for the Bible as God's record of his loving activity in reclaiming man for fellowship in the family of God; experience as a pastor or member of the ministry staff of more than one church; training experience as pastoral ministries leaders in seminars and workshops; and writing experience as authors of articles and books with wide circulation among Southern Baptist church leaders.

Walter Bennett is pastor of Lakeside Baptist Church in Lakeland, Florida. A native of Monroe, Louisiana, he earned degrees from Baylor University, Southern Baptist Theological Seminary, and Vanderbilt University. Bennett has held membership in the Association of Clinical Pastoral Education. As an employee of the Sunday School Board of the Southern Baptist Convention, he was a consultant in pastoral ministries and design process specialist/Church Program Training Center coordinator in the Church and Staff Support Division. Prior to joining the staff of the Sunday School Board, Bennett was pastor of churches in Kentucky and Illinois.

Robert D. Dale is associate professor of pastoral leadership and church ministries at Southeastern Baptist Theological Seminary. A native of Neosho, Missouri, he earned his Ph.D. from Southwestern Baptist Theological Seminary for graduate study completed there and at Kansas University. He is tration Department. Before joining the staff of the Sunday School Board, Ishee served as minister of education and associate pastor of two Kentucky churches. In addition to having written lesson and devotional materials for a number of Sunday School Board periodicals, he has written the teaching aids for several church study course books, including *Principles of Stewardship Development, Guiding Adults, Understanding Adults, Rope of Sand with Strength of Steel, Colossians: Christ Above All,* and *Romans: Everyone's Gospel.* He is author of three Broadman books: *From Here to Maturity, When Trouble Comes,* and *To Possess a Dream.* He is also editor of the Broadman book, *Is Christ for John Smith?*

Reginald "Reggie" McDonough, a native Texan, is secretary of the Church Administration Department. Before joining the Board's Church Administration staff in October 1964, McDonough was minister of music and education for over three years at North End Baptist Church, Beaumont, Texas. Prior to that he was instructor of religious education at East Texas Baptist College in Marshall. Earlier, he served as minister of music and education at First Baptist churches in Thibodaux and Arcadia, Louisiana. McDonough is a bachelor of science graduate of East Texas Baptist College, Marshall, and earned his master of religious education and doctor of education degrees at New Orleans Baptist Theological Seminary. In addition to editing *Church Administration* magazine and church administration materials for several years, he has written articles for numerous denominational publications. *Working with Volunteer Leaders in the Church* was published by Broadman Press in 1976.

Ernest E. Mosley, a native of Arkansas, is supervisor of the Pastoral Section, Church Administration Department of the Sunday School Board. Before coming to the Sunday School Board, Mosley was pastor of the University Avenue Baptist Church, Honolulu, Hawaii. He holds the bachelor of arts degree from Ouachita Baptist University and a master of divinity degree from Southwestern Baptist Theological Seminary. His service as pastor, assistant pastor, and education director of churches has taken him to Texas, Arkansas, Louisiana, and Hawaii. Mosley has served as president of the Hawaii Baptist Convention and chairman of that convention's long-range planning committee. He is author of *Called to Joy: a Design for Pastoral Ministries, Priorities in Ministry, The Up Side of Down: Helps for Hospital Patients, The Deacon Family Ministry Plan,* and coauthor of *Vocational Guidance in a Church.*

## Notes

[1] Ordway Tead, *The Art of Leadership* (New York: McGraw-Hill, 1935).

[2] A. Donald Bell, *How to Get Along with People in the Church* (Grand Rapids: Zondervan Publishers, 1960).

[3] Wayne E. Oates, *The Christian Pastor* (Philadelphia: Westminster Press, 1951).

[4] Brooks R. Faulkner, *Getting on Top of Your Work* (Nashville: Convention Press, 1973).

# 1

# Moses: Leadership That Overcomes Obstacles

Walter A. Bennett

Among biblical leadership profiles, Moses provides a valuable model. In any record of progress in the redemptive purpose of God, this man must be given careful consideration. Moses was regarded by the first-century Jews as the greatest man who ever lived. They measured Jesus against Moses as their standard (John 6:30 ff.). The writer of Hebrews went to great lengths to show that Jesus was mightier than Moses (Heb. 3:3).

It would be unreasonable to list the ten greatest men in biblical history without including Moses. If the apostle Paul excelled all others who lived after Christ, certainly Moses towered above all who walked the earth prior to Christ. The words which were appended to Deuteronomy after Moses' death support this: "And there arose not a prophet since in Israel like unto Moses" (Deut. 34:10). Stephen's comment concerning Moses in the book of Acts speaks volumes: "And Moses . . . was mighty in words and in deeds" (Acts 7:22).

In Moses we can see some of the qualities that ought to characterize any Christian leader but particularly the minister—one who is given a specific place of leadership in a church. Valuable lessons can be learned from the way Moses related to the task God gave him, as well as from the way he related to the people with whom he worked in seeking to accomplish the task. He surrounded himself with followers whose talents and efforts were supportive. The result was a strengthened and enlarged ministry for both Moses and his colaborers.

There are two kinds of leaders: "if" leaders and "however" leaders. The first type leader is often paralyzed by the size or difficulty of the task before him. Unable to act decisively, he spends his time daydreaming about what he could do *if* certain circumstances were different. He is often heard to wish: "If I had more staff, I could . . . . If I had some trained, capable lay leadership, I could . . . . If the church debt were not so great, I could . . . . If the people were more committed, I could . . . ."

The other type leader is fully aware of the obstacles before him, but he is committed to action. He begins decisively where he can, with what he has at his disposal. He is often heard to say: "We could use more staff; however, we are involving our deacons and other leaders in a shared ministry. We do not have many trained lay leaders now, but we have begun an intensive training program that will change that."

Moses is an example of the second type leader. He faced great obstacles; but as a man of action, he moved decisively against those things that confronted him. He may not have always acted appropriately, but he did act.

Within Saint Peter in Chains Cathedral in Rome

stands Michelangelo's renowned statue of Moses. Though seemingly perfect in every detail, it has a piece of stone chipped from one knee. The story is told that when the great sculptor had completed his work, he stepped back to appraise it. So life-like did the statue appear that Michelangelo impulsively struck its knee with his hammer exclaiming, "Why don't you speak to me!" The statue is only a lifeless replica of the man; a search of the biblical account of Moses will reveal the man and his leadership style.

What are the elements that made for greatness in this man? In his writing on Moses, Herschel Hobbs noted three. First, he possessed a God-given capacity for greatness. Second, he lived in an environment which gave opportunity to express greatness. Third, he was surrounded by lesser men who contributed to his greatness. These three elements were important; but ultimately, Moses was great because he had a great God working in and through him.[1]

Moses was called of God to serve in a difficult place of leadership. He faced great obstacles in the accomplishment of the task to which he was called. Some of these difficulties were handled well; others were not. Both Moses' successes and his failures provide valuable examples for the Christian leader today.

The real test of any leader often comes at the points of stress caused by difficulty in getting tasks accomplished. A look at how Moses handled difficult situations provides the framework for this study.

## Dealing with Opposition

No leader likes opposition. There is something inside each of us that makes us want to be at peace with others. Yet the nature of the leadership task involves a high potential for conflict. The minister's role often demands that he be a change agent. The biblical images of change are that of salt, light, and leaven. Change means the disturbance of the *status quo.* It often means challenging the values and commitments of the group which result in conflict and opposition.

This was Moses' experience. First, he experienced opposition from Pharaoh, who had little sympathy for the idea of releasing the Jews. Pharaoh saw no reason to give up a valuable source of free labor, and he certainly had no sympathy with the Jewish belief in Jehovah God (Ex. 5:2-5).

How do you as a leader deal with opposition when it is unbelieving, unyielding, and perhaps even threatening to your safety? Moses found the courage to stand firm and to proclaim the message of God without hesitation (Ex. 8:25-29; 10:3,24-26). Where does such courage come from? It comes from a firm conviction of who God is and the awareness of one's relationship to God.

No doubt Moses had many occasions that prompted him to review his call. He reminded himself again and again that he did not choose to be where he was but that God had chosen him and promised to be with him. The "I AM" had promised to accompany him and to sustain him

(Ex. 3:14). Moses' words would be the words of God (Ex. 4:12). God would not suffer his purpose or his chosen instrument to fail.

There surely must have been moments of discouragement and doubt (Ex. 5:20-23). In the midst of the plagues, Pharaoh's heart seemed to be unyielding and his will unbending (Ex. 7:14,22; 8:15,19,32; 9:7,34), but Moses was strengthened by his faith in the supreme power of God and the ultimate achievement of his purpose (Ex. 6:1-9). In any age the man of God will be sustained by his belief in the sovereignty of God, by his personal call to ministry, and by the clear understanding of the task that is before him.

Note also that Moses experienced opposition from his own people. Opposition from an unbelieving world, while often difficult to endure, is understandable; but opposition from the people of God can be a heavy burden. Pharaoh's response to Moses' demands that he let Israel go increased the burden of the Jews. They were required to make the same number of bricks per day but now had to furnish their own straw. The response of the people was to accuse Moses: "See what you have done, Moses. You have put a sword in Pharaoh's hand to kill us" (see Ex. 5:21).

Has that kind of situation happened to you? Have you felt resistance from the very people you were trying to help? Why did they oppose you? Do you understand the factors in their resistance?

Did resistance occur because they had suddenly become aware that to achieve the goal would require sacrifice, even hardship on their part? Or was it that they had not yet made a commitment to do what must be done to accomplish the task? How could you as a leader have helped them to make that commitment?

Was their faith in God small, capable of growing, but at the present, a faith that had difficulty believing that God could and would ultimately achieve his purpose? What could you have done to help them increase their faith?

Did they fear the unknown or question their ability to do the thing that was before them? How could you as their leader have helped them to become more comfortable with the change that they were experiencing and would experience? Was the anxiety compounded by the fact that you were a new leader and they were not yet comfortable in their relationship with you? Had they had sufficient time to develop confidence in your leadership? How could you have helped them at this point?

### Dealing with Delays

Another obstacle Moses confronted in his leadership was frustration caused by the delays in accomplishing his task. The distance between Egypt and the Promised Land was only about two hundred miles. It should have been an easy journey of twenty days; yet it took the Israelites forty years to make the trip.

One of the greatest challenges a leader faces is his ability to deal with what ought to be and what is—the tension between what a group of people is capable of doing and what they, in fact, do.

How does a leader handle his frustration and

disappointment when the people are not as committed to the mission of the church as they ought to be? or when the church does not grow as it should? Do his sermons and interpersonal relations reflect his anger and disappointment? Does he use guilt and threat to coerce the people? If he does, will he ultimately alienate the people and jeopardize his leadership?

In Exodus 15 through 17 Moses dealt with this same problem. He is pictured as the patient leader of a people with little faith (Ex. 16:8,16-20). The people murmured at every inconvenience (Ex. 15:24; 16:2-3). They had experienced the deliverance of God through the plagues and the Red Sea, but they could not trust God for the daily needs of the journey in the wilderness.

Can you accept your people where they are and as they are? Are you willing to walk them at a pace they can follow? Are you willing to accept them even if it means some detours along the way?

James L. Sullivan, past president of the Sunday School Board, has a helpful analogy of leadership. He compares leadership to using a rubber band. The leader must exert enough pressure to create a pull forward but never to the extreme that would cause the band to break.

Moses displayed a firm commitment to the people and to the task. Again and again we see him standing between the people and God. He was alternately the spokesman for God bringing to the people the message he had received (Ex. 19:7; 24:3) and the intercessor coming to God on behalf of the people seeking mercy and forgiveness (Ex. 32:31-32).

In the journey from Egypt to Israel there were delays and detours. Moses had to be able to adjust. He showed the patience and tolerance of spirit to overcome and to move forward in achieving this task.

## Dealing with Untrained People

What a motley, disorganized mob it must have been that crossed the Red Sea into the wilderness. The Jews had been slaves in Egypt. There they had had neither the opportunity nor the will to organize themselves into a nation. What an awesome task it was for Moses to undertake to lead them through the desert.

The fears and murmurings of the people are all the more understandable when seen in the light of their background. Their years in slavery had reduced them to a sustenance level of existence where food, shelter, and escape from the whip were the basic goals of life. As slaves, discipline had been imposed from without. Now they must exercise the self-discipline demanded of a free people.

In the wisdom of God, the wilderness provided the setting for Moses to transform the Jews from a mob into a nation which was capable of taking and occupying the Promised Land. The laws of God were revealed to them (Ex. 20—23) and adopted by them (Ex. 24:3). The people were organized, and leadership was selected (Ex. 18:21-23;

Num. 11:16-17). Both the civil and religious life of the people were instituted.

A pastor once said to me: "I have no leaders in my church. I have no one who is capable of assuming and carrying out a leadership role." Yet this pastor also revealed that he had been with the same congregation for twenty years. His statement was not a judgment of his people but rather of his ministry.

One of the functions of the minister-leader is to help persons discover, develop, and use their gifts. As a minister helps others to see their gifts, he is able to share the work of ministry with them. The gift of the pastor-teacher, according to Ephesians 4, is equipping the people of God for the work of ministry. The minister who is not training people is mortgaging his future and the future of the church. The investment he makes in training others is one upon which he will draw interest throughout all of his ministry at the church.

## Dealing with the Seemingly Impossible

The fact that the Jewish people were disorganized and untrained caused Moses to lose his perspective at one point. Exodus 18 records the visit of Jethro, his father-in-law, with Moses in the wilderness. Jethro rejoiced at the deliverance of Israel out of Egypt, but he was troubled by what he saw his son-in-law doing. From morning to evening, Moses was busy with the administrative duties of leading the nation. The people stood in long lines throughout the day to seek his counsel.

"Why are you trying to do all this work by yourself?" asked Jethro. "What you are doing is not good for you or the people. The needs of the people are not being met, and you will do harm to yourself" (see Ex. 18:14,18). Then Jethro suggested a plan for arranging the people and dividing up the responsibility of administering the nation (Ex. 18:19-23). It is to Moses' credit that he could listen to good advice.

It is bad when a leader becomes isolated and cut off from his people. It is even worse when they do not feel that they can come to him with information or the leader does not feel the need to listen when they do try to share information with him. The effective leader realizes the need for feedback and makes provisions to get it. In this way he keeps his blind spot at a minimum.

Moses acted decisively on the advice of Jethro. He learned to share responsibility. He was able to give others both responsibility and the authority to act. He trusted others. As a result he developed a large number of persons who were also leaders, including his successor Joshua.

Each pastor or staff member must face up to the impossibility of his task. If he is sensitive to the needs of the church and the people, he knows he cannot do all that needs to be done. There are two ways to deal with the impossibility, yet necessity, of the task.

First, the leader must have a clear sense of his priorities. Not everything he does is of equal value to the church. Therefore, he must try to do those things which are most important and will show the greatest return for the energy invested. If a leader clearly understands his own priorities, he can say yes or no when appropriate and not feel guilty.

Second, a leader must learn the value of delegation. Delegation is a way for the leader to multiply his effectiveness. Consider five types of responsibilities that can be shared with others:

1. Anything that someone can do better than you.

2. Anything that someone can do instead of you.

3. Anything someone can do at less expense than you.

4. Anything that someone can do with better timing than you.

5. Anything that will enable that person to grow in Christian maturity.

## Dealing with Anger

Sometimes the biggest obstacles the leader has to overcome are those inside himself. So it was with Moses. Numbers 20 records Moses' experience in striking the rock at Kadesh. By this time in the wilderness journey, the sequence of events was familiar. There was no water, and the people complained to Moses. Moses interceded with God. God commanded Moses to speak to the rock, and the water that was needed would be provided. But instead Moses struck the rock, not once, but twice. The water came forth as promised, but God was not honored in the experience. Perhaps Moses was tired or impatient with the people's lack of faith. The burden of leadership may have been particularly heavy that day; it could have been the realization that the journey was going to be longer and more difficult than he had imagined. Whatever the reason, anger and impatience prevailed; and God was not honored.

The lesson here is that a leader can lose his self-control, but there is a price to be paid, and God will not be glorified in such a situation. For Moses the price was great. Neither he nor Aaron would be able to enter the Promised Land with Israel.

The effective leader must know how to deal with his emotions. He will experience a whole range of feelings both positive and negative. He must know how to handle the feelings that come when things are not going well—the stress that is caused by disappointment, delays, misunderstandings, and even opposition.

There is always a danger that a leader's pent-up anger or frustration will build up until it explodes. Persons and causes may be hurt by the explosion. The result of such behavior is often broken relationships and the loss of confidence in the leader.

Here are several suggestions to help in dealing with anger:

1. Take responsibility for your own emotions. Do not blame others for your feelings or actions. If you get angry, it is because you choose to do so. You are responsible for any actions arising out of your feelings.

2. Learn to deal with anger in a constructive manner. Look for appropriate ways to work out your anger through work, problem-solving, and release through play. Do not underestimate the value of recreation in the release of tension.

3. Learn to deal with anger in each experience then and there. You should not allow unresolved anger to build up in your life. A meaningful daily devotional life can be a valuable help in dealing with anger. Jesus said, as he taught about overcoming worry, "Sufficient unto the day is the evil thereof" (Matt. 6:34). The truth applies to anger as well.

## Dealing with the Failure to Succeed

What does a leader do when it becomes evident that he will not be able to achieve his ultimate goals? Despite the investment of forty years in the life of the nation, Moses would not be able to lead them into the Promised Land. He would come close, but someone else would lead the people across the Jordan.

Most leaders are persons of vision. They can see a situation as it is, but even more important they can see a situation as it can become. A good leader makes an investment in the future. He believes that he can help people be more than they are, perhaps even more than they thought they were capable of being. In other words, the effective leader must be a person of faith.

The Christian leader serves out of his commitment to God, but he also gets some personal satisfaction out of seeing his dreams become reality. Conversely, a leader is also disappointed when those dreams go unrealized. If that happens, what do you do? Do you get angry and accuse others? Do you pout and play the martyr? Do you quit trying? Do you leave? Do you question God?

How these questions are answered may reflect

a leader's attitude about success. What constitutes success in leadership? If a leader has a limited definition of success, one that demands ultimate victory, such as leading the people all the way into the Promised Land, then he would have to label Moses as a failure. But if successful leadership can be seen as containing these elements—faithfulness to the purpose of God, a combination of patience and challenge that continually moves the people forward, a daily faithfulness to the task that walks step by step with the people, and the laying of a foundation that can be built on by those who follow—then Moses was a success.

Few leaders achieve all their goals whether professional or personal, but it is imperative that a leader have a sense of God's purpose about his life. It is also imperative that a leader sense movement toward those purposes day by day in his life.

One of the measures of a leader is how he relates to adversity; for adversity, as much as any other one thing, reveals the character of a leader. Moses was called of God to a task that involved facing many obstacles. Some of the obstacles were within himself, and others were external to him. He handled some of these obstacles better than others. But Moses was a man committed to God and committed to his task. He faced each difficulty in the strength of those commitments.

### Note

[1] Herschel Hobbs, *Moses' Mighty Men* (Nashville: Broadman Press, 1958), pp. 1-2.

# 2

# Joshua: Leader
# in His Own Right

Brooks R. Faulkner

Like Barnabas and Paul, Joshua trained under the shadow of a prominent man, Moses. Joshua was identified as Moses' *minister* (Josh. 1:1), meaning "a special assistant or lieutenant." He was a special assistant or lieutenant to the "servant of the Lord" (Josh. 1:1), the loftiest title used in the Old Testament for any man.

Joshua's leadership profile may have become partly obscured because it is often overshadowed by Moses' prominence.

While Moses' leadership style certainly deserves attention, modern-day leaders should also give careful study to one of the most attractive models in the Old Testament—Joshua. He did much more than fight the battle of Jericho.

Picture the historical setting. Moses had accomplished the dramatic acts of history: the punishment of the Egyptians by the plagues, the freedom of Israel, the parting of the Red Sea, and the dramatic presentation of the Ten Commandments. How does one replace a leader with those credentials?

Southern Baptists have had similar occurrences. How do you replace a W. O. Carver, a George W.

Truett, an R. G. Lee, or a Billy Sunday? Where do the Joshuas come from?

Strangely enough, there always seems to be a Joshua. A leader will emerge to replace a great leader. When George Truett died, he seemed irreplaceable. Yet W. A. Criswell has been no less a leader. When Billy Sunday died, the world of evangelism had a great void; but Billy Graham filled that void. A Joshua seems to emerge when there is a need for a new Moses.

### His Introduction to Leadership

The first time Joshua is mentioned in the Bible is when, as Israelite general, he fought in the battle against Amalek (Ex. 17:8-16). This was the exciting and romantic account of Moses' having his hands held up by Aaron and Hur. As long as Moses' hands were held up, Joshua continued to win over Amalek.

He also participated in the representation of the tribe of Ephraim in the spying out of Canaan (Num. 13:8,16). With Caleb, he argued that the land could be taken. This account is a foreshadowing of the great courage Joshua was to display.

Even the name *Joshua* deserves attention. It is used interchangeably with Hoshea, Jehoshua, Oshea, and Jehoshuah. The Hebrew word literally means "salvation." [1] The name *Joshua* has the same derivation as the name *Jesus.*

Before Moses' death Joshua was commissioned as his successor (Num. 27:18-23; Deut. 31:7-29). "And Joshua the son of Nun was full of the spirit of wisdom; for Moses had laid his hands upon him:

and the children of Israel hearkened unto him, and did as Jehovah commanded Moses" (Deut. 34:9, ASV).

## His Commission

Joshua had the same commission as did Moses. In fact, he is often thought of as a second Moses. He had the presence of Jahweh, as Moses did: "There shall not any man be able to stand before thee all the days of thy life: as I was with Moses, so I will be with thee; I will not fail thee, nor forsake thee" (Josh. 1:5, ASV). Joshua was admonished to be strong and of good courage. "Only be strong and very courageous, to observe to do according to all the law, which Moses my servant commanded thee: turn not from it to the right hand or to the left, that thou mayest have good success whithersoever thou goest" (Josh. 1:7, ASV).

## His Authority

Joshua was obeyed as was Moses. He won the respect of the people. He proved himself. "According as we hearkened unto Moses in all things, so will we hearken unto thee: only Jehovah thy God be with thee, as he was with Moses. Whosoever he be that shall rebel against thy commandment, and shall not hearken unto thy words in all that thou commandest him, he shall be put to death: only be strong and of good courage" (Josh. 1:17-18, ASV). That kind of respect demanded no small responsibility.

God's annointment was obviously upon Joshua. When Joshua took his forty thousand armed sol-

diers across the Jordan (Josh. 3:7 to 4:14), the people were reminded of God's anointment on Moses
as demonstrated in the crossing of the Red Sea.
The flow of the Jordan stopped. The people crossed
over on dry ground, just as they did over the Red
Sea. "Israel breaks camp near the ford of the Jordan and sets out in prearranged order, the Ark
in the lead, to cross over (v. 14). The crossing occurred in the time of harvest which, in the lower
Jordan Valley, comes in April. This was also the
season when melting snows on Mount Hermon
caused the Jordan to flood (v. 15). The Jordan flood
made the act of God all the more spectacular." [2]
The account of Joshua's direction over the Jordan
was no less miraculous than the dramatic account
of the crossing of the Red Sea.

There were also reminiscences of Moses' burning bush experience. "And the prince of Jehovah's
host said unto Joshua, Put off thy shoe from off
thy foot; for the place whereon thou standest is
holy. And Joshua did so" (Josh. 5:15, ASV). The
episode becomes especially significant to biblical
scholars and historians because it is another theophany, a rare occurrence in the biblical accounts
of God's people. A *theophany* is "an appearance
or self-revelation of God. Therein God was understood to be genuinely present in an audible and
visual manifestation, which varied with the setting and circumstances of the experience." [3] The
importance of the theophany in the biblical account of Joshua is that God revealed himself in
this manner to so few persons. Joshua had become
supremely regarded by the biblical writers be-

cause of this phenomenon.

There is a certain royal aura about the figure of Joshua in the Old Testament accounts. He is seen as one who has the "spirit." "And Jehovah said unto Moses, Take thee Joshua the son of Nun, a man in whom is the Spirit, and lay thy hand upon him" (Num. 27:18, ASV). *"Spirit* designates a special capacity endowed by God. The laying on of hands here represents the transference of power on assumption of office. Spirit of itself was not enough; there must be a particular appointment and a reception of special grace for a special task." [4]

Another significant occurrence about Joshua was the changing of his name. In Numbers 13:16, Moses changed his name to Joshua from Oshea. This practice occurred when the personage took on a royal air. The similarity was seen also in the changing of names from Jacob to Israel.

Joshua also had judicial powers and responsibilities. In Joshua 14:6-15, he is called on to decide claims. This function was usually isolated to the responsibilities of a king.

### His Leadership as a Staff Member

Joshua's first official responsibility was as a spy. He and Caleb decided that the land of Canaan could be taken. "And Joshua the son of Nun and Caleb the son of Jephunneh, who were of them that spied out the land, rent their clothes: and they spake unto all the congregation of the children of Israel, saying, The land, which we passed through to spy it out, is an exceeding good land.

If Jehovah delight in us, then he will bring us into this land, and give it unto us; a land which floweth with milk and honey. Only rebel not against Jehovah, neither fear ye the people of the land; for they are bread for us: their defence is removed from over them, and Jehovah is with us: fear them not" (Num. 14:6-9, ASV).

The other spies were cautious. "We cannot possibly complete this task," they told the people of Israel. They said, "We are not able to go up against the people; for they are stronger than we" (Num. 13:31, ASV). These people could have been acting out these roles just as credibly in a church today. Caleb and Joshua could just as easily have been the staff minister presenting a ministry plan to the church leaders. Moses and Aaron could just as easily have been the pastor and associate pastor. They could have been listening carefully and attentively as Caleb and Joshua with youth and idealism explained that the ministry plan would work. In fact, they insisted, it is a responsibility we cannot afford to pass up. It is in God's plan, so they feel. The objective is clear. God has brought Israel out of the land of bondage and into the land of milk and honey. However, it is the responsibility of God's people to act as if they have the commission from God. It is dereliction of duty to back off at this late date.

A deacon suggests that the church has tried a similar plan before. It didn't work. The pastor and associate pastor listen with concern. The deacon had been with the church for decades. He had seen the successes and failures. He had been right many times before. Caleb and Joshua could have begun to back away from their proposal. They were appointed commissioners from the responsible leaders. They certainly would not want to alienate those who had appointed them, but they stuck by their original suggestions. We do have the strength. We can conquer the land. The ministry plan will work if we believe that it is of God's design.

To run the risk of failure is a courageous act. The risk is doubly dangerous when one is in the minority. The risk is even more elevated when one has not had opportunity to prove himself in other arenas. More than likely this was Joshua's first major assignment. If Moses had chosen not to adhere to the advice of Joshua, it could have impaired Joshua's effectiveness with other leaders.

Several lessons in leadership can be learned from this episode:

First, it is important to run the risk. If a leader believes in taking positive action, he should stand behind what he believes in. However, he should be prepared to fail. In other words, he should have already given himself permission to fail. He should feel that after he has given his best it is OK if he fails. But running the risk is important.

On the other hand, running the risk is not enough. Just giving the minority report is only the beginning. Joshua needed someone to stand behind him after he had run the risk. If a staff member in a local church runs the risk of sticking his neck out when he believes in something, it is sweet to have the support of the person supervising him.

In the case of the staff minister, it is good to have the support of the pastor. In this case, Moses supported Caleb and Joshua's report. Then the report had much more clout with the elders of Israel.

An interesting facet to Joshua's personality almost slips up on the reader in Exodus. "And Jehovah spake unto Moses face to face, as a man speaketh unto his friend. And he turned again into the camp: but his minister Joshua, the son of Nun, a young man, departed not out of the Tent" (Ex. 33:11, ASV). In the verses that follow, an intimate conversation between Jehovah and Moses takes place. Joshua, remember, had not left the room. Moses then requested, "If I have found favor in thy sight, show me now thy ways, that I may know thee, to the end that I may find favor in thy sight: and consider that this nation is thy people" (Ex. 33:13, ASV). This is a significant learning experience for Joshua. Moses was showing him the most intimate side of his nature. He was giving Joshua the opportunity to see him at his most vulnerable moment. He was asking for favor from God. He was seeking out the blessing. He was saying, "Lord, don't let me lose face in front of these people." Has any serious minister failed to pray that prayer in one way or another in his ministry?

Moses did not insist that Joshua leave the room. Moses could have insisted that all the underlings leave the room as he carried on this important priestly and intimate function with Jahveh. He did not; he permitted the young son of Nun to stay in the room and share the mission.

The fact that Moses did not insist that Joshua

leave the room is a great study in motivation. Moses knew that if Joshua stayed he would see Moses pleading. When one pleads, he loses much of his dignity unless there is great respect from those who serve with him. When great leaders see the clay feet of other great leaders, the experience does not lessen their sense of mission but, rather, increases it. Joshua saw that Moses was vulnerable and seeking. He also knew that Moses had permitted him to see him in this manner. He knew that Moses would never see the Promised Land because he had been disobedient in striking the rock instead of speaking to it as God had commanded him. Now Moses was again communicating with God, negotiating a place of strength for himself with his (Moses') people. Seeing the clay feet of their leaders does not lessen the ambition of great men. It did not lessen Joshua's respect for Moses to see him in this manner.

A church in Texas was blessed with a large staff. The daughter of a pastor found it necessary to seek treatment for a drug problem. Surely that situation could have become an opportunity for a disgruntled staff member to be disapproving of the pastor. Instead the pastor brought the staff into the delicate family problem. They prayed about it together. The staff supported the pastor. Soon the situation became better. The young lady was treated redemptively by both the staff and the church. The result of this incident was that both pastor and staff gained mutual respect for each other. A large staff was even more blessed as a result of this difficult problem. The staff did not have less respect for the pastor; they had more. The pastor had trusted them implicitly, and they had supported him. They had acted in behalf of the Christian faith. They continued to share their Christian mission.

Joshua was a faithful and loyal staff member. He was prepared to become the leader with the ultimate responsibility of Israel. One of the principle reasons was the trust that Moses placed in him by permitting him to see his own vulnerability and humanity.

## His Leadership as Head of Israel

Moses' work was completed. He had taken the children of Israel out of the land of bondage. It was time for a new breed, and Joshua was of that new breed. He was not particularly young. Tribble, Hill, and Yates, wrote that he was perhaps "forty years of age." [5] He had successfully led the forces of Israel against the Amalekites in Rephidim (Ex. 17:8-16); he had accompanied Moses into the mount of God (Ex. 24:13); and he had remained constantly in the tabernacle while Moses went out into the camp (Ex. 33:11). He had known the value of intimate contact with the incomparable Moses. He was ready!

Successful leaders have support; they have support from having been commissioned to a task, and they have support from having been affirmed as a person. Joshua had both.

"And Moses did as Jehovah commanded him; and he took Joshua, and set him before Eleazar the priest, and before all the congregation: and he laid his hands upon him, and gave him a charge, as Jehovah spake by Moses" (Num. 27:22-23, ASV). The Hebrew people placed special emphasis on the blessing. The account of Jacob and Esau seeking the blessing of their father, Isaac, is an example. Ancestral approval was necessary for peace of mind. The blessing gave a symbol of the commission. Moses realized the importance of the blessing, and so did Joshua.

Much has been made in our time of the good and bad effects of parental influence. Some leaders become distorted in their effectiveness because they are trying to prove themselves to a superdisciplining parent. Long after the father or the mother is gone, the son or daughter still behaves in ways that have been shaped by the blessing or the lack of blessing from their parents. A popular entertainer is the son of a minister. Recently on a late-night talk show, he spent some five minutes talking about the importance of forgiveness in their family relationships. He indicated that his own life had been shaped in such a manner that it was virtually impossible for him to hold a grudge. It seemed to him to be a waste of energy. He felt his father had molded this behavior for him. The father had given him the "blessing" of forgiveness of others.

A blessing indicates that you are worth something. Joshua must have felt the meaning of this blessing from Moses. He had this communicated to him in a ceremony. This ceremony is still a popular activity in today's churches. It is the "laying on of hands." We impart a blessing by the laying on of hands. It is a popular agenda item in the ordination of ministers and deacons.

In a Personal and Professional Growth Course, a pastor from Virginia told the story of his own ordination. He had been ordained over twenty years prior to his relating the incident. He said: "I have forgotten all the words. I, unfortunately, have even forgotten some of the persons who took places of responsibility in the ordination. However, I will never forget the feeling I had when those thirty-five or forty men laid hands on me. Never had I felt so unworthy and yet so affirmed. It was a paradox. I felt both small and large. I felt small because the task was so monumental. I felt large because all of that power from so many of God's men was implanted into my skull, at least symbolically, through the laying on of hands."

Effective leadership must have been blessed. God must bless the effective leader, and other men must convince the leader that God has blessed him. That is what Moses did. He convinced Joshua that God had blessed him and commissioned him to be the leader of Israel.

The curse of effective leaders is *comparison.* Where would Israel find another Moses? They would not, of course. Throughout his ministry Joshua would serve under the aura of the stories of Moses. Every pastor has felt some part of this phenomenon. To some church members the former pastor becomes more and more lovable after he has gone. At least, it seems that way to the succeeding pastor. He must listen, as patiently as possible, to the stories of how the former pastor visited

every member in the church at least three or four
times per year. Each time he made a tactical move,
Joshua must now hear the generals and the cap-
tains of the armies of Israel tell of the formidable
tactics of Moses. It would be especially difficult
for him to find his own unique and special gifts
of leadership. The difficulty would be magnified
because Joshua himself had emulated the leadership and ministry of Moses.

There are at least two ways to succeed an effective leader. The successor can virtually destroy the
organization in which the former leader worked.
He can build his own regime. That is one way of
succeeding a predecessor. The second possibility
of succeeding an effective leader is to build on his
strengths. Both could work, or neither could work.
It depends on the circumstances and situation in
which the leader finds himself. Joshua chose the
second alternative. He decided to build on the
strengths of Moses. But what strengths did Moses
have to build on?

Joshua must have felt that Moses had both position and personal power. Amitai Etzioni said that
the difference between position power and personal power springs from the concept that power
is the ability to induce or influence behavior, that
power is derived from an organizational office,
personal influence, or both. "An individual who
is able to induce another individual to do a certain
job because of his position in the organization is
considered to have position power, while an individual who derives his power from his followers
is considered to have personal power. Some indi-

viduals can have both position and personal power." 6 Moses had both position and personal power. But what power did Joshua have?

First of all, Joshua was given the position power. Moses did that for him in commissioning him by the laying on of hands. Joshua would be the official leader of Israel at the appointment of Moses.

He had to earn his personal power through identifying his own special gifts. Personal power is the extent to which followers respect, feel good about, and are committed to their leader, and see their goals as being satisfied by the goals of their leaders. Joshua had not proved himself. The only history he had with his followers was as a spy and as a successful general. He had given evidence of his strength, but he was still to prove that he had warmth. Most followers look for both in their leader. An example is the reservations expressed by the American people in the election of Dwight D. Eisenhower as president. His credentials were excellent. The only reservation, which was consistently voiced, was, "Can he feel our pain?" Fortunately for the American people, he had both the strength and warmth.

Joshua had the powerful weapon of the Word of God. He listened attentively as the Lord said to him: "Joshua, This day will I begin to magnify thee in the sight of all Israel, that they may know that, as I was with Moses, so I will be with thee. And thou shalt command the priests that bear the ark of the covenant, saying, When ye are come to the brink of the waters of the Jordan, ye shall stand still in the Jordan" (Josh. 3:7-8, ASV). Often

God's leader must recall his most powerful weapon; he has been given the shield of God, and he must act as if he carries it. Joshua decided that he had been given that admonition, and it was time for him to act as if he had been given that admonition.

A leader who searches for his own personal gifts must not forget the power which comes in being one of God's men. He is called; he is appointed; and he is admonished to act as if he has been both. In the struggles of leadership, loneliness is often a disturbing barrier. The leader often feels as if he is the only one left. Elijah exclaimed, "It is enough" (2 Sam. 24:16). Many of us have felt, "That is all I can take." Leaders must remember that God has not left them. They are not alone. It was those signals that God was giving Joshua in the passage in Joshua 3:7-8. Do not dismay. Moses is gone, but God is not. The former pastor may have left his mark. He may still have loyalties that will last for several decades, but God is here, and he will not forsake you.

Joshua was given both position and personal power. Each pastor who assumes leadership must remember that he has been given the position power both from the calling of the church and from the calling of God. He must earn the personal power by winning the respect, admiration, and commitment of his church members. They must realize that their own goals are being realized through his leadership, and that will call for sensible and democratic leadership.

## His Example as a Leader

Most Christian leaders will never lead an army out of Egypt. On the other hand, most will not succeed Moses or anyone like him. However, there are a number of things Joshua did in his leadership from which leaders can learn. These things are as relevant today as they were during the historical context of the Old Testament.

*1. Courage.*—With Caleb he risked his own credibility at a time that was crucial. It was crucial for the people of Israel, and it was crucial for future credibility with Moses. An effective leader cannot function durably without courage.

*2. Opportunity.*—An effective leader seizes the moment. Moses had been reprimanded by God. He had been disobedient. He was not privileged to lead the people of Israel into the Promised Land. Joshua was handed the responsibility from Moses. He could have become emotionally reluctant, but he didn't. He seized the moment. He looked for ways to complete the task as God had intended. He knew that the opportunity was right for him.

The historical significance of a leader's effectiveness may be the highest priority. In other words, his effectiveness may well depend on his ability to feel the pulse of history. "Now is your time" feelings are prevalent among successful politicians. This may have been true of Joshua; it may be true of ministers who seize the moment and know when to act. Their awareness of timing may ultimately determine their effectiveness.

*3. Clout.*—Joshua had power. He had gained position power and personal power from his predecessor. He was given an admonition from God. He had the clout necessary to execute his strategy for victory. An effective leader must have clout. The church must give it to a minister; but, conversely, the minister must earn it. He should not shrink from it but use it with responsibility and tenderness. It is naive to believe that clout is not a necessary part of determining a leader's effectiveness.

*4. Sense of direction.*—Joshua knew where he was going. He had a vision of the direction to Canaan fixed in his mind, and he was willing to lead his people into that land. He kept his sense of direction in mind as he stopped the flow of the Jordan for the people to cross on dry ground (Josh. 3:14-17).

A minister must have a sense of direction if he is to lead effectively. The world follows those who know where they are going. Those who do not know where they are going will either follow or step out of the way. A sense of direction is vital.

*5. Sense of mission.*—A leader must have a sense of mission. Joshua knew what his mission was, to lead God's people into the Promised Land. The first five chapters of Joshua prepare the reader for the seige of Jericho told about in Joshua 6:1-27. God was with the people. The mission was accomplished as the walls collapsed. The city was then captured and occupied. Any pastor who has been through a successful vote to begin construction of a major building must know a little of the victory felt with those people at Jericho.

*6. Ability to live with shades of gray.*—One last characteristic is important in the study of the biblical model of Joshua. He was able to live with the shades of grey. He was certain to have been confused about why Moses was not allowed to lead the people of Israel into the land of Canaan. However, he was obedient to God. He had some unanswered questions, but these unanswered questions did not deter him from his direction and sense of mission. Here is an important lesson for ministers. Some of the most loving and tender churches come from the hurts and pains of church fights and disturbances. It is confusing to the discerning and compassionate. It is, nevertheless, one of the unanswered questions effective ministers must live with.

Joshua did fight the battle of Jericho. He succeeded Moses and did it with flair and fanfare. He was one of God's chosen. He listened and learned under a great teacher. He administered his gifts with love and responsibility.

## Notes

[1] E. M. Good, "Joshua," *The Interpreter's Dictionary of the Bible,* E-J (New York: Abingdon Press, 1962), p. 996.

[2] William H. Morton, "Joshua," *The Broadman Bible Commentary,* Vol. 2 (Nashville: Broadman Press, 1970), p. 314.

[3] Ibid., p. 320.

[4] John Marsh, "The Book of Numbers," *The Interpreter's Bible,* Vol. 2 (New York: Abingdon-Cokesbury Press, 1953), p. 273.

[5] H. W. Tribble, John L. Hill, and Kyle M. Yates, *Old Testament Biographies* (Nashville: Broadman Press, 1935), p. 144.

[6] Paul Hersey and Kenneth H. Blanchard, *Management of Organizational Behavior* (Englewood Cliffs, N. J.: Prentice-Hall, 1972), p. 92.

*Resources*

Pfeiffer, Robert H. *Introduction to the Old Testament.* New York: Harper and Row Publishers, 1948.

Tribble, H. W., Hill, John L., and Yates, Kyle M. *Old Testament Biographies.* Nashville: Broadman Press, 1935.

Wood, Irving F. *The Heroes of Early Israel.* New York: Macmillan Publishing Co., 1920.

# 3

# Elijah—Can a Prophet Be a Leader?

Leadership is always a function of personality in environment. The environment influences the personality, and the personality alters the environment. Thus, evaluation of leadership effectiveness always must be done with this transactional reality in mind. This transactional influence is obvious in the leadership patterns of Elijah.

## The Character

The Scripture gives us only glimpses of Elijah's appearance. "He wore a garment of haircloth with a girdle of leather about his loins" (2 Kings 1:8, RSV).[1] Apparently, this dress had a uniqueness about it that was characteristic of a unique personality. Elijah, the Tishbite—that's what he was called. He grew up in the rugged mountain country east of Jordan. He absorbed into his character the rugged individualism that such an environment usually produces. Elijah's personality developed amid afflictions and hardships of life in that lonely, mountainous terrain. Out of a stressful environment God shaped a leader for one of the greatest crisis periods in Hebrew history.

49

## The Culture

When the Hebrew nation divided in 722 B.C., Jeroboam became king of the Northern portion, which continued under the name of Israel. The greater and Southern portion of land, Judah, became the possession of Israel and maintained the primary religious and cultural influence. Jerusalem, with its Temple and holy days, was the unifying cultural influence for all the Hebrew people. Jeroboam, in an effort to unify the people of the north, erected a golden calf for people to worship. Probably, Jeroboam would have denied that he had ceased to worship and serve Jehovah. More likely is the possibility that the erection of the golden calf was an "ecumenical" endeavor to merge the symbol of the Canaanite religion, Baalism, with the worship of Jehovah. Thus, Jeroboam hoped to unite his people and diminish their interest in the holy heritage of Jerusalem.

The writer of the book of Kings made it clear that Jeroboam's apostasy made Israel sin. His example seemed to have been followed by the kings that succeeded him until Ahab ascended to the throne. Ahab made no attempt to maintain any semblance of the worship of Jehovah. Rather, Ahab took a new departure from the practice of Jeroboam when he built a temple and set up an altar to Baal. The sin of Jeroboam was a violation of the Second Commandment, that of making a graven image to represent or symbolize God. The sin of Ahab, however, was a flagrant repudiation of the First Commandment—that of replacing Jehovah God with the god of his choosing.

Ahab was assisted in his sordid efforts by his wife, Jezebel, a pagan queen who seemed to be guided by few moral principles and inhibited by no fear of God or man. She sought to "evangelize" Israel with the worship of Baal.

Baal worship was not a new phenomenon in Israel. Baalism was a Canaanite religion encountered by the Hebrews when they possessed the Promised Land. Baal was the god of fertility, and part of the act of worship was to perform immoral sexual acts in the temple.

It was into such a cultural situation that Elijah came to fulfill his "calling of confrontations." Four confrontations stand out in the survey of Elijah's work.

### The Confrontations

The first confrontation occurred between Elijah and Ahab. In the midst of this abominable culture, Elijah appeared before Ahab and made a startling announcement: "As the Lord God of Israel liveth, before whom I stand, there shall not be dew nor rain these years, but according to my word" (1 Kings 17:1). Such a confrontation would have been a task too great for a coward and too volatile for a hothead. It required a man who was neither an appeaser nor an aggressor. Rather, the situation called for the appropriate amount of assertion— a firm stand without fury.

After making the pronouncement, Elijah dropped out of sight as far as Ahab was concerned. For three years he was secluded from Ahab, and for three years it did not rain. One can imagine that when Elijah first made his announcement, it was received with something less than seriousness; but as the dust became more prevalent and the streams began to dry up, Elijah's pronouncement began to be taken with greater seriousness. It was because he was taken seriously that he was able to achieve the second confrontation—the contest with the prophets of Baal on Mount Carmel. Three years after his first appearance, Elijah challenged Ahab to a showdown at Mount Carmel. Ahab was to send four hundred fifty prophets of Baal to "do battle" with Elijah and his God. " 'Let two bulls be given to us; and let them choose one bull for themselves, and cut it in pieces and lay it on the wood, but put no fire to it; and I will prepare the other bull and lay it on the wood, and put no fire to it. And you call on the name of your god and I will call on the name of the Lord; and the God who answers by fire, he is God.' " And all the people answered, "It is well spoken" (1 Kings 18:23-24, RSV).

The biblical description of the contest is dramatic. First, the writer described the futile attempts of the prophets of Baal to get a response from their gods. Next, he told how Elijah sarcastically "teased" the prophets of Baal with the idea that their god " 'is musing, or he has gone aside, or he is on a journey, or perhaps he is asleep and must be awakened' " (1 Kings 18:27, RSV).

Then Elijah's time came. He built an altar and drenched it with water. He then prayed a simple but sincere prayer. "Then the fire of the Lord fell, and consumed the burnt offering, and the wood, and the stones, and the dust, and licked up the water that was in the trench. And when all the people saw it, they fell on their faces; and they said, 'The Lord, he is God; the Lord, he is God' " (1 Kings 18:38-39, RSV).

Elijah enjoyed his triumph. He relished in his victory. He had won! At least, he thought he had. Surely now Ahab and Jezebel, as well as all the Hebrew people, would reject Baal and turn to Jehovah. They might even proclaim Elijah a hero. Elijah sent word to Ahab, " 'Prepare your chariot and go down, lest the rain stop you' And in a little while the heavens grew black with clouds and wind, and there was a great rain" (1 Kings 18:44-45, RSV).

Quickly, Ahab left Mount Carmel and drove his chariot to Jezreel. "And the hand of the Lord was on Elijah; and he girded up his loins and ran before Ahab to the entrance of Jezreel" (1 Kings 18:46, RSV). Twenty miles—that's how far Elijah ran! Moreover, he outran Ahab's chariot. Here was one Hebrew prophet who could run. Spurred by the desire to claim his victory, Elijah went to Ahab's palace. Here his third confrontation occurred.

When the fate of the prophets of Baal was told to Jezebel, she sent word to Elijah: "So let the gods do to me, and more also, if I make not thy life as the life of one of them by tomorrow about this time" (1 Kings 19:2). When Elijah heard these words, his valley became as low as his mountain was high. Fear struck his heart, and he ran. Finally, in a desert place he stopped and poured out his feelings of depression before God. At Carmel

Elijah was prepared to win, but he was not prepared to lose. His loss led him into a deep depression.

The fourth confrontation was a confrontation with God: "And, behold, the word of the Lord came to him, and he said unto him, What doest thou here, Elijah?" (1 Kings 19:9). Elijah talked to God about how he felt. The process placed Elijah on the road to overcoming his depression. He experienced a renewal of hope. Elijah anointed Hazael to be king over Syria. He appointed Jehu to be king over Israel. And, he anointed Elisha to be a prophet. Elijah's hope was renewed, and his Spirit began to heal.

## The Conclusions

What can be learned about leadership from the analysis of Elijah's life and ministry? Several lessons seem apparent.

*Appropriate assertion.*—An effective leader needs to learn how to be appropriately assertive. Appropriate assertion is at the midpoint on a continuum that ranges from appeasement to aggression. Thus, appropriate assertion may be illustrated as follows:

Appeasement          Appropriate          Aggression
                          Assertion

Each of the three points on this continuum are typical of various types of leaders.

The characteristics of the appeaser include allowing other people to make most decisions, even if the consequences of the decisions appear to be negative. Thus, the appeaser seldom achieves desired goals, because the goals of other people become dominant over his own goals. The appeaser seeks to become what other people want him to become or implies that he agrees with other people when he does not. He does this as a means of gaining acceptance and minimizing disapproval. He becomes like the chameleon that changes color to blend in with the environment.

The appeaser runs the risk of losing his integrity. *Integrity* means "wholeness." The word comes from the mathematical term *integer,* which is a number that isn't divided. A person of integrity isn't divided against himself. He doesn't think one thing and say another. He doesn't believe one thing and do another. He is not in conflict with his own principles. Integrity is the absence of inner warfare, which enhances one's ability to act consistently. When integrity is absent, there is division in the inner kingdom. Jesus said, "If a house be divided against itself, that house cannot stand" (Mark 3:25). Winston Churchill once commented, "An appeaser is one who feeds a crocodile—hoping it will eat him last."

At the other end of the continuum is the aggressive leader. The aggressive leader insists in making most decisions himself. He may achieve his goals, but his leadership style tends to alienate people. Thus, in the long run the aggressive leader may lose his followers.

The assertive leader strikes a good balance between appeasement and aggression. Not that the diagram provides for a wide range of assertive behavior. At times, assertion needs to be either lesser or stronger, depending on the issue and the people involved. The assertive leader tends to be democratic in the decision-making process. He expresses his opinions and listens to the opinions of others. Thus, decision making involves negotiation with people in an effort to hear the opinion and respect the rights of both leaders and followers. Decision making becomes a practice of the priesthood of the believer.

*Appropriate timing.*—There are three kinds of time. All three are gifts from God.

The first of these is *chronos* time. *Chronos* time is calendar time, the ticking of the clock, the rising and setting of the sun. It cannot be accumulated like pennies or stockpiled like the winter supply of fireplace wood. It cannot be turned on and off like the television set or replaced like the worn-out family car. One does not manage *chronos* time, for the minute hand is beyond control. It moves relentlessly on. *Chronos* time passes at a predetermined rate no matter what one does. People cannot manage the clock; they can only manage themselves with respect to the clock. Thus, the consideration of how persons use their time brings them into confrontation with an array of problems related to self-management.

The second kind of time is *kairos* time. In contrast with chronos or chronological time, kairos time is the "right" time, the fullness of time. This is the time Jesus referred to when he said, "The time is fulfilled" (Mark 1:15). This same meaning of time was expressed by Paul when he stated, "When the fulness of time was come, God sent forth his Son (Gal. 4:4). Kairos time is providential time that focuses on God's preparation and man's response in significant events and circumstances. Kairos time is God's movements in marvelous ways to bring about the opportunity for persons to respond.

The third kind of time is *experienced* time. Experienced time is the way we manage or respond to chronos or kairos time, the way we perceive time. Sometimes experienced time seems to rush by especially when time is filled with pleasure. In other circumstances experienced time drags by. Moments seem like hours when waiting for word from the physician who is performing surgery on a loved one.

We cannot change chronos time. It is fixed into God's laws of nature. Moreover, we cannot control kairos time; we can only be open to God's revelation so that we may be aware of kairos moments and respond to them appropriately. We can, however, change to a great extent the nature of our experienced time.

Kairos time is the appropriate time for something to happen. God creates it, and the good leader recognizes it. Elijah's second confrontation with Ahab was at the kairos moment. The rain had not fallen for three years, just as Elijah had prophesied. Imagine the degree of credibility Elijah had gained. Now Ahab would listen. Now Elijah could issue a challenge to the prophets of Baal and not be ignored.

I recall with pain of regret the first church that I pastored. The congregation had outgrown its building. I was aggressive in trying to convince the deacons that we should build. We did need to build. I realized that. What I did not realize was that the time was not right. The kairos moment had not come. I could get no response from the "power people" in the congregation. Twenty years later I drove through the church community and noted that the one rural church had become suburban. I also noted the new building erected beside the old one. The kairos moment had come, and the people had responded. Waiting for kairos is not being passive; it is being attuned to God working in his world to create moments of possibility. Kairos is letting the river flow by itself, rather than trying to push it.

*The reality of defeat.*—The leader who aspires to make a significant contribution will experience both victories and defeats. Many times his defeats will follow closely on the heels of his greatest victories. The valleys will become as low as the mountains were high.

Elijah experienced depression. The circumstances surrounding his depression reveal the causes and treatment of his problem.

The cause of Elijah's depression is clear. First, he was a victim of unrealistic expectations. Following the duel with the prophets of Baal on Mount Carmel, Elijah assumed that he had won the support of his opponents, the leaders of the nation.

Second, he was threatened with loss of life. "And Ahab told Jezebel all that Elijah had done, and withal how he had slain the prophets with the sword. Then Jezebel sent a messenger unto Elijah, saying. So let the gods do to me, and more also, if I make not thy life as the life of one of them by to morrow about this time" (1 Kings 19:1-2). Jezebel's message exploded Elijah's illusion of victory. The necessity of returning to reality contributed to his depression.

Third, Elijah was tired. His energy-draining confrontation with the prophets of Baal at Mount Carmel had left him in a state of physical exhaustion. His depression is clear in his statement, "It is enough; now, O Lord, take away my life; for I am not better than my fathers" (1 Kings 19:4).

The cure for Elijah's depression was two-fold. First, God provided him with food and rest (see 1 Kings 19:5-8). Second, God provided him with the occasion to talk about his depression. "And, behold, there came a voice unto him, and said, What doest thou here, Elijah?" (1 Kings 19:13). Elijah talked about how he felt.

This process placed Elijah on the road to overcoming his depression. He experienced a renewal of hope. "So he departed . . . and found Elisha . . . and cast his mantle upon him" (1 Kings 19:19). Elijah's choice of Elisha as his successor was an expression of his hope that his cause would live on.

No one is exempt from the possibility of depression. When confronted with it, one can find his strength again by recognizing the depression and seeking to deal with it constructively and forthrightly.

Most people move through periods of depression

to states of renewed normality. Such low periods are normal in the face of a perceived loss. In fact, if a person suffers a loss and does not experience at least some measure of depression, he may be deceiving himself. Furthermore, he may be inviting a delayed reaction to the loss. Delayed reactions are often more difficult to deal with because it is harder for the person to identify the cause of his depression.

The first step in dealing with depression is to "own" it. Such a statement may seem absurd. However, the fact is that people often deceive themselves into thinking that they can bear the loss without becoming depressed. People who see depression as a sign of human weakness or a lack of faith in God may deny their depression, but to deny the pain of depression is to encourage lack of treatment.

The second step in dealing with depression is to try to bring into focus the cause of the depression. The causes of depression often are blurred to the person experiencing it. To bring into focus probable causes of the depression often requires a high degree of objectivity—something the depressed person may not possess. The process of trying to identify causes of depression is an exercise that helps a person gain this objectivity.

The third step in dealing with depression is to talk about it with a trusted friend. Talking about one's feelings is functional in helping the person to (1) own the feeling, (2) explore alternatives about the causes of depression, and (3) move out of a state of immobility to a state of action. Talking about one's feelings is an activity that helps to unify the three areas of life—the mental, the emotional, and the physical. When these three areas of life are integrated, the person's will or ability to determine direction becomes stronger.

*The source of strength.*—God is the Christian leader's source of strength. The genuine power of a leader is power that is a gift from the Holy Spirit. "You shall receive power when the Holy Spirit has come upon you" (Acts 1:8, RSV). Every leader will experience defeat, but defeating circumstances can become a sanctuary where the Christian leader rediscovers the reality of God and his need for him.

Elijah knew both the joy of victory and the agony of defeat. He made mistakes, but he also made a contribution. He learned as he lived and led. In so doing he received the privilege of sharing God's glory.

### Note

[1] From the Revised Standard Version of the Bible, copyrighted 1946, 1952, © 1971, 1973. Subsequent quotations are marked RSV.

*Resources*

Ishee, John. *From Here to Maturity.* Nashville: Broadman, 1975.

———. *To Possess a Dream.* Nashville: Broadman, 1977.

Wood, Fred. *Bible Truth in Person.* Nashville: Broadman Press, 1965.

# 4

# Nehemiah: Builder
# of Walls and People

Ernest E. Mosley

"And at the dedication of the wall of Jerusalem they sought the Levites in all their places, to bring them to Jerusalem to celebrate the dedication with gladness, with thanksgivings and with singing, with cymbals, harps, and lyres. . . . Then I brought up the princes of Judah upon the wall, and appointed two great companies which gave thanks and went in procession. . . . So both companies of those who gave thanks stood in the house of God, and I and half of the officials with me; . . . and the singers sang with Jezrahiah as their leader. And they offered great sacrifices that day and rejoiced, for God had made them rejoice with great joy; the women and children also rejoiced. And the joy of Jerusalem was heard afar off" (Neh. 12:27,31,40,42-43, RSV).

The majestic excitement in the sounds of celebration found in Nehemiah 12 is likely to be felt by any reader who recalls the discouraging testimony the travelers gave Nehemiah, recorded at the beginning of this chronicle: "And they said to me, 'The survivors there in the province who escaped exile are in great trouble and shame; the wall of Jerusalem is broken down, and its gates are destroyed by fire' " (Neh. 1:3, RSV).

The book of Nehemiah nears its end (Neh. 12) with the songs of praise and thanksgiving accompanied by sacrificial gifts joyously presented, characterizing the celebration of the people of Jerusalem. How does a nation of people move from trouble and shame to gladness and singing? The restored Sheep Gate, Fish Gate, Old Gate, Valley Gate, Dung Gate, Fountain Gate, Water Gate, Horse Gate, East Gate, and Muster Gate all help to make the wall secure and functional. What forces could change Jerusalem's image from that of broken down, gateless walls to a securely walled city with ten guarded gates? The processional of chapter 12 moved upon the walls and through the gates where frightened inhabitants once huddled in fear and shame. How could such a change occur?

The answers to these questions are not found in some sudden upturn in political, economic, or social circumstances. Throughout the account Judah remained a captive land. The restoration was accomplished in spite of the awareness that a similar effort had recently been stopped by King Artaxerxes as a threat to the security of his kingdom (Ezra 4). The economy had not experienced an upturn that favored the people. They were concerned with getting grain and staying alive, with having enough money to pay the king's tax, and with keeping their children from slavery. Nor had the hostility of their neighbors been changed to goodwill. To the contrary, every gate was restored, every section of the wall repaired, and every song of celebration sung to the background sounds of the jeers, threats, and ridicule of angry and enraged neighbors (Neh. 4:1-3,7-8; 6:1-9).

In the face of all of the indicators of failure, people were united, the work completed, and their accomplishment celebrated. It was because a man named Nehemiah was willing to become a leader. He was willing to be as weak or as strong, as submissive or as controlling, as fearful or as brave as effective leadership required. He became a leader in order to help his people regain their respect through the rebuilding of their city's walls.

Nehemiah was moved in his heart to become the leader in restoration. Through his effective leadership the people of Judah were moved to pay the price in personal and corporate effort to once again become the victorious people of God. Through his leadership the people of Judah were able to overcome obstacles that seemed insurmountable. They heard again the joyful sounds of celebration because God called out a leader to show the people how to climb out of failure and into success.

Who was this leader? What made him different from those who failed to lead the people to the celebration? What can be learned from him that is applicable to the search for success in leading God's people today?

The key words that describe Nehemiah, the builder, are *faith, action, skill,* and *tenacity.* The first letters of these descriptive words, seen as an acrostic, are FAST—suggestive of the remarkable feat of rebuilding the walls of Jerusalem in fifty-two days. That feat surfaces the genuine pride and joy of the people of Judah when they saw what could be accomplished through working together to achieve the goals that belong to these people of God.

## The Builder of Walls Is a Person of Faith

Biographical data about Nehemiah is sparse. His father was Hachaliah. He was a descendant of the tribe of Judah and probably of the royal family of David. If his character had been shaped by his lineage, the biblical record would likely have given more attention to family lines. Instead, he is introduced as one of the Jews in exile, one who had a responsible service position as cupbearer to Artaxerxes Longimanus, king of Persia.

*Nehemiah's effectiveness as a leader in Judah was not influenced so much by his ancestry as by the quality of faithfulness that characterized his service.*—This faithfulness is evident from the time he is first introduced. The king cared for him enough to be sensitive to his sadness and to be concerned about its source (Neh. 2:2). One would expect this response only if the servant had expressed devotion to his king in faithful service.

When Nehemiah's concern had been expressed in a bold request, King Artaxerxes granted what he asked (Neh. 2:5-8). This response is all the more dramatic when viewed in the light of the king's earlier command that Rehum and Shimshai stop the rebuilding and refortification of Jerusalem (Ezra 4:8-23). The faithfulness and integrity of his cupbearer had impressed the king. God had used qualities of a servant to prepare the king's will for sending Nehemiah back to Jerusalem with letters assuring safe passage and a supply of materials for use in rebuilding the walls. Nehemiah's experiences are remindful of the words of Jesus in the parable of talents, "Well done, good and faithful servant; you have been faithful over a little, I will set you over much" (Matt. 25:21, RSV).

Leadership qualities are shaped more by environment and training than they are by the heritage of power or prestige. When Jesus began to do his work, many among the masses could not get beyond such questions as "Can anything good come out of Nazareth?" (John 1:46). It is more important to look for personal faithfulness to God's purpose and plan than to look for heritage or position as qualifications for effective leadership.

*Nehemiah demonstrated faith in the promises God had given his people in the past.*—The history of Old Testament Judaism looked like roller-coaster centuries of successes and defeats. Whenever the children of Israel and Judah remembered their relationship to God and obediently honored the relationship, success was celebrated. Defeat and humiliation were always associated with forgetting their heritage and following after the heathen gods of new neighbors. A basic reason Nehemiah could lead the people back into the joy of success was because he had a holy sense of history. Days of exile and years of service to a foreign king had not lessened his commitment to the "Lord God of heaven, the great and terrible God who keeps covenant and stedfast love with those who love him and keep his commandments" (Neh. 1:5).

As his prayer continued, Nehemiah recalled God's command to Moses (v. 8). Victory for Moses and the people was contingent on their faithfulness to God's commands. Nehemiah was in full awareness of this episode in the life of Moses. With historical support that God wanted to give success to his servants, Nehemiah called out in faith to God and then spoke out boldly before King Artaxerxes.

Effective leadership in the kingdom of God in any century, leadership that does not glow to catch attention before burning out like a falling star, depends on a consciousness of the stream of history. Moses moved out in the awareness that "I AM has sent me to you" (Ex. 3:14, RSV). Joshua's leadership reflected this awareness of God at work through man. In the midst of the struggles involved in occupying the land God promised his people, the chronology is recorded: "As the Lord had commanded Moses his servant, so Moses commanded Joshua, and so Joshua did; he left nothing undone of all that the Lord had commanded Moses" (Josh. 11:15, RSV). A New Testament example is seen in Stephen's stirring message to the people in Jerusalem. His allegiance to Jesus was likened directly to "the God of glory [who] appeared to our father Abraham" (Acts 7:2, RSV).

Leaders who maintain awareness of their relationships to the God of Abraham, Isaac, and Jacob, as well as to the God who will one day "wipe away every tear from their eyes" (Rev. 21:4, RSV), will be able to lead their people in faith. The events of which they are a critical part will always be viewed in the larger picture of God's victorious movement through history.

This awareness of the God of history enabled Nehemiah to understand what God wanted him to do. He knew that God would not be inconsistent, that he would keep his promises to the people. He "told no one what my God had put into my heart to do for Jerusalem" (Neh. 2:12, RSV), but he moved boldly into a difficult task with faith that God had a plan for the present and sufficient power for each day. Christian leaders are characterized by such boldness when they are aware that their work is consistent with God's plan and that their strength is sustained by the power of God.

Nehemiah's boldness before King Artaxerxes and before the enemies around Jerusalem is like the courage of Esther before King Ahasuerus and his lieutenant Haman. She responded with a sense of personal mission when her uncle, Mordecai, said, "And who knows whether you have not come to the kingdom for such a time as this?" (Esther 4:14, RSV). Like God's great leaders throughout history, those who master the challenge in this age do so out of a sense of personal mission, an awareness that God has equipped them for the tasks which are uniquely theirs. Nehemiah's confidence is felt in his words, "the good hand of my God was upon me" (Neh. 2:8, RSV), and "the God of heaven will make us prosper" (Neh. 2:20, RSV). Nothing can bolster a leader in preparing for a difficult task, sustain a leader in the face of frustration and seeming defeat, or give proper perspective to a leader experiencing the flush of victory as much as the awareness that God is at work in his world. We are privileged to be God's servants in helping his kingdom to come on earth as it is in heaven.

The minister whose activity is characterized by faith will not only inspire the people of the church to follow, but he will also cause the people around the church to notice that God's people are different. Some of the people who have been skeptics or enemies of God's people are led to become people of faith themselves when they have observed the results of faithfulness to God. Nehemiah recorded that his enemies were afraid and lost their self-esteem because they perceived that the work they had been resisting was actually accomplished "with the help of our God" (Neh. 6:16, RSV). The other side of the valley of struggle for Christian leaders may be the great satisfaction of seeing those who have made the work difficult respond to faithfulness by acknowledging the power of God and perhaps even exercising their faith in God.

### The Builder of Walls and People Is a Person of Action

Bold faith becomes reality only in terms of action. Foy Valentine put it together in the book *Believe and Behave.*[1] The apostle James said, "So faith by itself, if it has no works, is dead" (Jas. 2:17, RSV). The record of Nehemiah's faith in God would be meaningless aside from the account of the way he moved to action to change circumstances. Monastic piety that analyzes faith and writes about it, without ever risking in the power of God to turn blight into beauty, is only a flight of fantasy. People of faith believe that the way is already provided by God and get busy turning dreams into action. Bold action is seen in at least five of Nehemiah's leadership events.

*Nehemiah went to the king.*—Though he was afraid, he made his petition to the king and boldly asked for generous support for the rebuilding of the walls of Jerusalem (Neh. 2:3-8). He was not among those who only practice speeches before the mirror, who fantasize boldness but are silenced by fear. The displeasure of Sanballat and Tobiah (Neh. 2:10) did not hinder him from getting on to the task.

Courage and boldness are never seen in people who simply dream dreams and see visions. The world applauds and follows those who take pen in hand and write, who move to the rostrum and speak, who go onto the playing field and compete, who mortar the bricks and build. Leaders must be dreamers, persons of vision; but the work of God among men will never be done until dreams are translated into action, until leaders put their lives on the line.

*He studied the conditions and quickly determined a course of action.*—The problem had existed long enough. Most of the people had either become too discouraged or too complacent to be effective in analyzing the problem and deciding on an appropriate course of action. Group participation and consensus in decision making are usually the most effective approaches for leading people to action. While it is true that people support best that which they help plan, sometimes they are unable to plan because of oppression or prolonged failure. Sometimes they cannot believe in the possibility of change enough to participate in deciding what to do. In these times a leader or leaders must awaken the people to initiative by taking action and pointing a way.

After a secret and thorough tour of the area, Nehemiah knew the conditions of the walls and the gates. He then called the people to follow him in a brave declaration of their faith in God by rebuilding the walls. His words were, " 'Come, let us build the wall of Jerusalem, that we may no longer suffer disgrace' " (Neh. 2:17, RSV). They were words that called for action out in the open. Obviously, those who did not want the walls rebuilt and Jerusalem restored to strength would see their work and oppose it. His call to action included hard labor and high risk.

The response of the people was to say, "Let us rise up and build" (Neh. 2:18, RSV) and to prepare themselves for the demanding task. It was as though Nehemiah had said to them, "We are no little people; ours is no little God; and this is no little task." The people in that day, just as they do today, were quicker to respond to a difficult job than they were to an easy one. People respond to challenge. To offer them a job that won't take much time, require much effort, or make much difference rarely gets an enthusiastic or prolonged response for able people. Nehemiah's challenge was big and bold, and people lined up to work with him.

*He involved himself with the people in the work*

*of building.*—The "let us'" language of Nehemiah was met with the "let us" language of the people. Though Nehemiah had just returned to Jerusalem from exile, he did not see himself as an outsider or a temporary sojourner. He belonged among the people and could use pronouns in the first person when he talked about their mission and the work to be done, as in Nehemiah 4:21: "So we labored at the work" (RSV).

Ministers who provide effective leadership to churches are most likely to do so by becoming personally involved in the mission of the church. They will think, speak, and act in terms of "our," "we," and "us." While the tasks they perform will usually be different from the tasks of others—they may be presiding over a planning council while others are running a bus route—they will be working with the people rather than merely ordering others' activities. While the evangelist or special emphasis speaker can be inspirational in helping a church accomplish its mission, the minister, who is felt by the people to be an ongoing part of the church, is in the best position to provide the most valuable leadership. And it need not take long for a leader to be received by the members as belonging.

*Nehemiah boldly confronted the nobles and officials who oppressed the people.*—Nehemiah 5 begins with the wailing of the people in a recitation of the acts of oppression to which they were submitted. Nehemiah's response was not a grin-and-bear-it lecture to the people. Rather, his emotion was anger, and his decision was to act. He confronted the responsible leaders with the facts and challenged them to begin to act rightfully. "So I said, 'The thing that you are doing is not good. Ought you not to walk in the fear of our God to prevent the taunts of the nations our enemies? . . . Let us leave off this interest. Return to them this very day their fields, their vineyards, their olive orchards, and their houses, and the hundredth of money, grain, wine, and oil which you have been exacting of them'" (Neh. 5:9-11, RSV).

The leader whose behavior gives evidence that he is guided and empowered by God does not need to be timid and fearful in the face of persons of power or persons of perverted values. Leaders should be known best in terms of what they stand for. Standing for some things usually means standing against other things. If one stands for justice, he must stand against injustice. If he stands for freedom, he must stand against slavery. If he stands for morality and the quality of life it produces, he must stand against immorality and the quality of life immorality produces. People will respect and work with leaders who are courageous and careful in taking action on their behalf.

*Nehemiah boldly ordered the keeping of the sabbath and the removal of those who defiled the priesthood.*—After a period of absence from Jerusalem, while he journeyed to Susa and spent some time with King Artaxerxes, Nehemiah returned to Jerusalem to find the religious life of the people in disrepair. His concern for their spiritual and national welfare caused him to turn Tobiah, the high priests' friend, out of the Temple and restore the room he had desecrated to its proper use. He restored the tithe and reorganized its use. He called the people back to keeping the sabbath, with a strong reminder of the price their nation had paid. "What is this evil thing which you are doing, profaning the sabbath day? Did not your fathers act in this way, and did not our God bring all this evil on us and on this city? Yet you bring more wrath upon Israel by profaning the sabbath" (Neh. 13:17-18, RSV).

Nehemiah had already made his mark as a leader. He had experienced more success than most people would expect in a lifetime, but his concern for the people would not let him rest on his laurels. The walls were built, but the people were not. His boldness in challenging those who led the people away from holiness was as important to building people as his boldness in building the wall.

## The Builder of Walls and People Is a Person with Leadership Skills

Faith and confident initiative are admirable qualities for leadership. They put a leader on the line and into the action. These essential qualities are not enough, however, because they may represent the spirit and action of only one person. Too many churches have experienced years of frustration and ineffectiveness even though their pastors were pious in attitude and diligent in effort. Frustration and ineffectiveness grew out of the pastor's lack of basic leadership skills. Growing people through the life of a church is much like growing people through rebuilding the city's walls. Organization is required; people must work together on common goals. The tasks must be discovered and described. People must be led to relate to tasks in ways that help the people grow and get the work of the church done. Interpersonal relations must be maintained so that trust grows and the work of one increasingly compliments the work of another.

In Robert Dale's chapter on Barnabas he identifies Barnabas as a 9.9 person, at the top of the scale on both task production and people relations (see chap. 6). This position is the peak of leadership effectiveness. The skills required to perform at this 9.9 level are evident in Nehemiah's dramatic experience in Jerusalem. To have rebuilt the walls of Jerusalem in fifty-two days is evidence enough of superior task production. This could be possible only through developing and maintaining a relationship of trust and confidence with the people. A study of Nehemiah's work and the people's response reveals skills in planning, motivating, delegating, setting priorities, communicating, and celebrating.

*Nehemiah began his work by surveying the needs and the possibilities.*—His plans for this major undertaking actually began even before that; for when he made his appeal to King Artaxerxes to be released and blessed for the work of rebuilding Jerusalem's walls, he also asked for resources with which to do the job. He did not rush into the work without counting the cost, which revealed the need for materials, a plan of action, and people willing to work to carry out the plan.

First, the materials were made available by grant of King Artaxerxes (Neh. 2:8). Next, the conditions were carefully studied to develop a strategy for changing them. While most plans for action should be developed by the people who are to implement the plans, the secrecy with which Nehemiah worked in developing his strategy seemed appropriate in view of the despair and disorder that characterized the people. His approach was justified. When he presented the plan of action to the people and invited them to join him (Neh. 2:17), they responded with enthusiastic commitment (v. 18).

Effective leaders take time to plan. They study the conditions of the community and the resources available to the people. They lead the people to set goals, to determine possible approaches to reaching the goals, and to decide on the strategies they will use in striving to accomplish the goals.

*Nehemiah challenged the people to possibility thinking.*—After helping them see their alternatives—continuing to suffer in disgrace or rising up to build the walls—he told them that he believed they could do it. God's promises were real to him, and he knew these people of God could do a great work. Not only did he tell the people that he believed in them, but he also told the critical neighbors that these were not ordinary people and they could prepare to watch these extraordinary people do an extraordinary job (Neh. 2:17-20). It is not surprising that this positive attitude, this affirmation of the worth of the people, is followed immediately by the solid sounds of construction activity (Neh. 3:1). The people went to work on a project that would give them healthy pride, security, and a sense of responsibility as the people of God.

Leadership theorists have focused attention on three kinds of people: those who make things happen, those who watch things happen, and those who say, "What happened?" Those who make things happen believe in people. They are, according to McGregor, Theory Y leaders. Theory Y leaders believe that people desire to accomplish, to get involved in constructive relationships and activity. They need opportunities. They need guidance and encouragement. This leadership attitude contrasts with the Theory X approach to leadership, which insists that people are basically lazy and have to be made to work.[2] Theory X leaders are likely to employ manipulation and control in trying to get the job done. Theory Y leaders will be motivators and, like Nehemiah, provide the necessary challenge, incentives, and support. The results can be like that recorded in Nehemiah 4:6: "So we built the wall; and all the wall was joined together to half its height. For the people had a mind to work" (RSV).

*Nehemiah organized the work and delegated responsibility for getting it done.*—Chapter 3 identifies the people responsible for repairing each section of the wall. All the people were given the opportunity to contribute to this significant enterprise. Among them were priests, Levites, Temple servants, rulers and their children, perfumers, goldsmiths, and merchants. Both men and women worked. People who lived inside the city and those from outside the walls were united in the effort. With this range of skills and with the scope of the job, it was essential that the work be organized and the specific parts of it delegated to persons who could be responsible for its completion.

Further evidence of Nehemiah's ability to organize the people for effective action is seen in Nehemiah 14. When it became apparent that the angry neighbors were determined to stop the reconstruction project, it was necessary for the builders to also become defenders. Nehemiah's wisdom did not allow him to take an either-or approach to the challenge. The construction had to continue while the defenses were maintained, both with no more personnel than was already at work. The solution was found in identifying the work to be done and assigning responsibility for it. "When our enemies heard that it was known to us and that God had frustrated their plan, we all returned to the wall, each to his work. From that day on, half of my servants worked on construction, and half held the spears, shields, bows, and coats of mail" (Neh. 4:15-16, RSV).

Major accomplishments in group endeavors require both those who can see the whole undertaking—all of its parts and how they relate to the whole—and those who can concentrate their attention on the tasks involved in one part of the whole. Churches need leaders who have peripheral vision, those whose mind can comprehend the big picture. These leaders can organize the work into appropriate components and assign the component parts to appropriate persons. This is organization and delegation. There is a significant difference between those who simply dream dreams and those who see their dreams become reality.

*Nehemiah kept priorities clear.*—He refused to be distracted by the invitation to fellowship with the enemies. The intentions of Sanballat and Tobiah were not clearly stated, but Nehemiah felt that "they intended to do me harm" (Neh. 6:2). Whether their desire was to lure him into a death trap or simply to distract him from his work through flattery, the results would have been disastrous. His repeated response was, "I am doing a great work and I cannot come down" (Neh. 6:3, RSV).

After Jesus was baptized and spent forty days in personal preparation for his mission as Son of God and Son of man, Satan approached him with propositions designed to alter his priorities. The real essence was not bread from stones or a spectacular leap from the Temple turret. Rather, the issue was service and sacrifice that would show people the nature of God. Voluntary death and triumphant resurrection would make it possible for people to be free from sin and return to fellowship with God. When Jesus said, "Begone, Satan! for it is written, 'You shall worship the Lord your God and him only shall you serve'" (Matt. 4:10, RSV), he set a priority management example for all Christian leaders. The price of success in the mission to which God has called church leaders includes strict adherence to priorities. There will always be challenging opportunities for capable people to turn aside from the work to be done and enter into alliances that promise success with fame or fortune. When leaders turn aside from priority tasks, laborers are left without support, walls go unmended, and the efforts of God's people fall short of the potential. Great leaders do not let inviting possibilities get in the way of critical priorities.

*Nehemiah kept the communication flowing with the people.*—He addressed them and instructed them in specific and forthright language. The opportunities and dangers were described honestly with words that kept everything out in the open. The record indicates that he stayed among them, worked alongside them, and kept on instructing and encouraging them.

The communication is clearly flowing in two directions by the time of the conversation that begins in Nehemiah 4:10. Nehemiah listened to his colaborers, and his attention was called to the failing strength of the burden bearers. His response was to adjust the strategy and to appeal to the people to continue to be courageous. Chapter 5 begins with a report of the people crying out for help in overcoming the injustices heaped upon them by those who controlled the land and kept them in economic slavery (Neh. 5:1-5). Nehemiah listened to the people, took their words seriously, and acted on their behalf. His leadership was on target because he encouraged two-way communication.

Some danger signals for ineffective leadership appear in phrases like: "I didn't know you had that in mind." "If I had known you felt that way, . . ."

"Why didn't somebody tell me?" The effective leader will be careful to speak clearly to the right people about the right things. He will also be careful to listen intently so that he may act responsibly.

*Nehemiah led the people to express joy and humility in celebration.*—Chapter 12 records the events of celebration, led by Nehemiah, in words like *gladness, thanksgivings, singing,* and *great joy* (RSV). "And the joy of Jerusalem was heard afar off" (Neh. 12:43, RSV).

The leader who guides people to great accomplishment can lead the procession of celebration. The accomplishments and the celebrations belong together. They encourage the people, and they honor God. Whether it is in the form of the dedication of a new building, a note-burning ceremony, a banquet honoring teachers and leaders who did their jobs well, or an evening of informal fellowship with friends, the people will continue to follow the leader who is as committed to the celebration as he is to the task.

### The Builder of Walls and People Is a Person of Tenacity

Dictionaries use words like "persistent," "strong," and "holding fast" to define *tenacity.* The writer of Hebrews appeals to Christians to "hold fast our confidence" (Heb. 3:6, RSV), and to " 'hold fast our confession' " (Heb. 4:14, RSV). Patience is not equal to tenacity; patience suggests enduring difficulty with a good spirit, while tenacity is persistence in pursuing the activity needed to change the conditions.

Nehemiah's leadership activity had the dogged determination called tenacity. When the situation got tough, his response was to get tougher, to look the problem squarely in the eye, and to take appropriate actions. This is not to imply that Nehemiah's emotional makeup was void of tenderness. There is no evidence that he ever blocked out his tender emotions and replaced them with total toughness. When, as an exile from his homeland, he heard of the conditions in Jerusalem, he reported that he "sat down and wept, and mourned for days" (Neh. 1:4, RSV). Nehemiah confessed to being afraid when he made his appeal to the king (Neh. 2:2). His prayer to God, after angrily throwing the household furniture out of the chamber in the house of God and remonstrating the officials, was "Remember me, O my God, concerning this, and wipe not out my good deeds that I have done for the house of my God and for his service" (Neh. 13:14, RSV). The healthy balance of tough-tender emotions did not allow Nehemiah to be vindictive and harsh, but they did equip him to stay with a difficult task and see it through to completion.

Leaders whose personalities have not been developed to include a healthy degree of roughness often respond to difficulties by running. Their response to confrontation is separation, isolation, and perhaps resignation. This response pattern has been ingrained in many leaders, during childhood and adolescence, by parent models, teacher models, and pastor models. A significant number of persons occupying leadership positions today observed that their parents responded to marital conflict by running to the divorce courts. Preadolescent children in Sunday School classes watched a processional of teachers coming to their class with great intentions and leaving in resignation because they could not gain control. Many grew up in church activity and became members of churches where pastors remained for no more than one or two years because they did not know how to handle the resistance and the conflict that invariably developed. Runaway responses become natural through such conditioning and often appear to be the only alternative.

Nehemiah's leadership profile is an example that may help leaders who are inclined to respond to the conflict situations in their lives with runaway tendencies. His tenacity models leadership behavior that is appropriate for builders of walls and people today. Think again about some examples of Nehemiah's response to conflict and compare them with your own experiences.

1. When Sanballat ridiculed the Jews and threatened to attack the construction project, Nehemiah led the people to pray for God's guidance. He organized a guard so the construction could continue (Neh. 4:1-9). The last verse of this chapter rings with tenacity: "So neither I nor my brethren nor my servants nor the men of the guard who followed me, none of us took off our clothes; each kept his weapon in his hand" (Neh. 4:23, RSV).

2. In the face of the social injustices that had been heaped on the people, Nehemiah called for

a drastic change. His prayer called for God to be tenacious with them if they did not change their behavior (Neh. 5:13).

3. When his counselors advised him to seek refuge by shutting himself within the Temple rather than to go on supervising the reconstruction project, his response was, "Should such a man as I flee? And what man such as I could go into the temple and live? I will not go in" (Neh. 6:11, RSV).

4. When the chronicle comes to a close, Nehemiah is still providing leadership for the people, helping them to maintain an orderly response to God. The tasks of leadership remained even after the walls had been restored and the joyous celebrations had ended. It is sometimes more difficult to stay on the job with the people when the struggles have ended and the battle has been won. Nehemiah's tenacity kept him among the people, helping them to live out the life of a restored people.

In spite of the successes Nehemiah experienced as he led God's people, he continued to wear the mantle of humanity well. Some who have looked back at Nehemiah from the perspective of New Testament revelation have judged him to be unforgiving and divisive. Some scholars hold him responsible for the deep and lasting divisions between the Jews and the Samaritans. Followers of Jesus don't recognize Christlike behavior in statements like, "I contended with them and cursed them and beat some of them and pulled out their hair" (Neh. 13:25, RSV). But Nehemiah is most often seen as a faithful human servant, asking God for guidance and power and taking on the difficult task of helping God's people claim their inheritance. His behavior, that might be judged harsh and abusive by the standards of mature Christians today, was gracious and gentle in comparison with the usual leadership behavior of his day. He could justifiably conclude his chronicle with the prayer, "Remember me, O my God, for good" (Neh. 13:31, RSV).

## *Notes*

[1] Foy Valentine, *Believe and Behave* (Nashville: Broadman Press, 1964).

[2] Douglas McGregor, *Leadership and Motivation* (Cambridge: M.I.T. Press, 1966), pp. 16-17.

# 5

# Paul: A Self-Actualized Leader

Reginald M. McDonough

With the single exception of Christ, the apostle Paul continues to be the most influential Christian leader of all time. Paul was a pioneer in taking the gospel to persons in lands far beyond the borders of Palestine. He was the principal writer of New Testament books. He was the premier bivocational preacher—preaching throughout the known world while making a livelihood from tentmaking. Not only did he establish churches throughout the Grecian world, but, as indicated in his letter to the Christians at Rome, he also desired to begin new work in Spain: "Now at last I am through with my work here, and I am ready to come after all these long years of waiting. For I am planning to take a trip to Spain, and when I do, I will stop off there in Rome; and after we have had a good time together for a little while, you can send me on my way again" (Rom. 15:23-24, TLB).[1]

What a vision! Paul was literally going to the ends of the known world to preach the gospel. This man of God was certainly a leader who merits serious study.

Both Paul's preparation for leadership and the characteristics of his leadership as compared to

Abraham Maslow's model of a self-actualized person deserve exploration.

## Preparation for Leadership

Through God's providence and a person's willingness to pursue training opportunities, every leader is endowed with experiences that can be used as preparation for leadership. Paul is certainly no exception. In Paul's early life he obviously had no idea of what God had in store for him, but it is apparent that the apostle to the Gentiles was being prepared for a unique ministry.

*Family heritage and early life.*—Paul, or Saul, was born in Tarsus, a Greek city in Cilicia (Acts 22:3). Paul's father was a Pharisee (Acts 23:6). The Bible is silent concerning his mother.

It is not known how or when Paul's family arrived in Tarsus. It is known that the Roman government awarded citizenship to certain Jewish craftsmen in exchange for their displacement from their homeland to various cities of commerce in the Roman Empire. Speculation has it that Paul's father was enlisted by the Roman government to move to Tarsus in return for citizenship. Paul's father was obviously a Roman citizen since Paul stated that he obtained his Roman citizenship by birth (Acts 22:28). As the son of a Pharisee, Paul was well educated in Jewish law and tradition. This family heritage and training provided a solid base from which he could build his Christian theology.

His childhood in Tarsus provided an important foundation for his work with the Gentiles. Tarsus

was geographically located at the crossroads of the
Mediterranean Sea and Syria. It was an important
center of commerce and learning. All types of religious cults were within easy reach in Tarsus. Paul
saw the best and the worst that Greek culture had
to offer.

Paul obviously spoke and thought Greek. The
Mars Hill sermon (Acts 17:22-32) proved that Paul
was certainly no stranger to the Greek world.

These foundational experiences in Paul's early
years provided important building blocks in the
development of his theology and leadership style.

*Education and fanatical devotion.*—Paul was
proud of his training at the feet of Gamaliel, a
well-known teacher of the rabbinical school in Jerusalem (Acts 22:3). According to custom, Paul
likely began his training in Jerusalem at about
age twenty. In his words he was "educated according to the strict manner of the Jews" (Acts 22:3,
RSV). He also gives evidence of being an extremely
zealous student. In Galatians 1:14, he stated, "I was
advancing in Judaism beyond many of my contem-
poraries among my countryman, being more extremely zealous for my ancestral traditions"
(NASB).[2]

Even here Paul was beginning to assert himself
as a leader. In fact, if Paul's student days had come
in the sixties, he would likely have been branded
as a student radical. Gamaliel, his teacher, was
known to be liberal-minded, as evidenced by his
own unwillingness to take a hard line against Jesus (Acts 5:34-40). Apparently this liberality did
not rub off on Paul. He described himself as "a

real Jew if there ever was one! What's more, I was a member of the Pharisees who demand the strictest obedience to every Jewish law and custom" (Phil. 3:5, TLB).

In these formative years Paul was developing a life-style of being totally committed to his cause. In his later ministry he drew on this mind-set many times.

*Arabian experience.*—In Galatians 1:16-17, Paul mentioned three years he spent in the Arabian desert. These days of meditation and study enabled him to prepare himself spiritually and mentally for his Christian leadership role. In addition to his devotional experiences, Paul likely put into focus his rabbinical training with his newfound revelation from Jesus Christ. It was in Arabia that Paul forged his Christian theology and strategy for ministry. The Arabian experience was undoubtedly an important part of Paul's preparation of leadership.

## Characteristics of Paul's Leadership

Paul is usually thought of as a hard-nosed, plainspoken leader with an intense determination to achieve his goals. Although every Christian leader would like to be as influential as Paul, few leaders have the gifts or the courage to copy his leadership style. Paul was an unusual leader with unusual gifts.

Abraham Maslow, a twentieth-century Jew, was also a person of unusual gifts. His psychological research has provided considerable insight into the human personality. Maslow, unlike many psychologists who base their studies on mentally ill persons, built his investigations around superior individuals. Through his studies and research of superior persons, Maslow has constructed a model of exceptional persons that he refers to as self-actualizers. This model has been selected to serve as a framework for studying Paul and his leadership characteristics.

Maslow defines a self-actualized person as an exceptionable person who's primarily motivated by the need to develop and actualize his fullest potentialities and capacities.[3] He believed the self-actualized person to be the best possible example of the human species. Paul's effectiveness as a Christian leader certainly justifies his consideration as a self-actualized person and leader. However, the use of Maslow's model to study Paul should not be seen as an attempt to validate Paul and his work. The New Testament is validation enough.

*Committed to a specific, meaningful mission.—* Without exception, Maslow found that self-actualizing persons were dedicated to some work, duty, or vocation which they considered important. For them, work was both exciting and pleasurable. Commitment to a major job is a major requirement for self-actualizers. The self-actualizing person also strives to do his work well. He is a person with a mission and is willing to give the hard work and discipline necessary to do it well.[4]

There were no New Testament leaders more committed to a specific mission than Paul. He repeatedly stated that his mission was to take the gospel to the Gentiles. In Acts 13:47, he and Barnabas stated: "For thus the Lord has commanded us, 'I HAVE PLACED YOU AS A LIGHT FOR THE GENTILES, THAT YOU SHOULD BRING SALVATION TO THE END OF THE EARTH' " (NASB). This was no casual statement. Throughout Paul's writings he makes numerous references to his calling to carry the gospel to the Gentiles.

The Scriptures make it clear that Paul's perception of his mission was accurate. Shortly after his conversion, Ananias was told in a vision that Paul was a "chosen instrument of Mine, to bear My name before the Gentiles and kings and the sons of Israel" (Acts 9:15, NASB).

Paul's ability to verbalize his Christian mission is a good lesson for Christian leaders today. The adage, "If you aim at nothing, you'll hit just that" applies here. A leader needs to know what he is about. This is not to say that a person who cannot state his mission is any less Christian or committed. It is not easy to verbalize one's mission. It takes hours of prayer, study, and identification of gifts and interests to sharpen the focus of personal mission. The matter can be pursued with several other Christian friends or through the increasing amount of literature being published today in which persons share the ways they have sought to identify their specific mission.

Significant also is the fact that Paul understood his mission to be specific. His particular ministry was directed to the Gentiles (Acts 9:15; 13:47; Rom. 11:13). This gave a focus to his ministry. His strategy was to plant churches and to nurture the new fellowships by return visits and written letters. There is a lesson for today's leaders here too. The more specific a person's understanding of his mission is, the more sharply focused his leadership goals and strategies can become.

*Concern for others more than self.*—Self-actualized persons are not ego-centered persons. One of their fundamental characteristics is that they concentrate on problems external to themselves. They are persons with a world view.[5]

Concern for other persons—Jew and Gentile— is the keystone of Paul's ministry. Perhaps his strongest statement in this regard is found in his letter to the Romans, "For I could wish that I myself were accursed, separated from Christ for the sake of my brethren, my kinsman to the flesh" (Rom. 9:3, NASB). Acts 20:24 also attests to his concern for others: "But I reckon my own life to be worth nothing to me; I only want to complete my mission and finish my work that the Lord Jesus Christ gave me to do, which is to declare the Good News about the grace of God." [6]

In 1 Corinthians 9:22 he said, "I have become all things to all men, that I may by all means save some" (NASB).

These represent only a few of the scriptural evidences of Paul's intense concern for others. No sacrifice was too great. He was willing to give his life that others might know Christ.

The lesson for Christian leaders today is plain; a Christian leader succeeds as he enables and equips others to grow in Christ's likeness. This is not to say that the leader should depreciate himself. In fact, for a leader to make a maximum contribution to others, he must have a healthy feeling about his own self-worth.

This, too, is not an easy lesson. A leader's understanding of himself is important. Because of his own feelings of insecurity and guilt, a leader is tempted to relate to others in order to meet his needs rather than theirs. History is filled with examples of leaders who have used their followers to build their own ego needs. Unselfish concern for others should be one of the distinctives of Christian leadership. Paul certainly exemplified this concern.

*Capacity for deep and meaningful relationships.*—Self-actualizers, says Maslow, are capable of more love and deeper relationships than most people.[7] This is likely true because they have a healthy self-esteem and are not easily threatened by others.

Although a person's first thought about Paul's relationships usually brings to mind his conflict with John Mark (Acts 13:13; 15:36-41), a deeper study shows that Paul was a person who established deep relationships. One of the best evidences of this capacity is his love for Timothy. In his first letter to Timothy, Paul called him "my true son in the faith" (1 Tim. 1:2, TEV). Again in his letter to the Corinthians, he expressed his feelings about Timothy: "For this reason I have sent you Timothy, who is my beloved and faithful child in the Lord" (1 Cor. 4:17, NASB).

Paul apparently had other close friendships with persons like Phoebe, Aquila, and Priscilla.

In his personal greetings at the close of the Roman letter (TEV), he used the term "dear friend" four times to refer to different persons. It is also interesting to note that Paul and John Mark were reunited, as reported in 2 Timothy 4:11.

A leader today also needs deep and meaningful relationships. His friends become his support system in time of celebration and in crises. They accept him as he is, not as they would like him to be. They give him honest feedback and genuine love. Although a self-actualized leader has the capacity to enjoy solitude, he greatly benefits from selective, deep, and meaningful relationships.

*Superior perception.*—Self-actualizers see life clearly. They have a clearer notion of right and wrong than the average person. They are far above average in their ability to judge people. With superior perception, they can see concealed and confused realities quickly and accurately.[8]

On several occasions Paul displayed superior perception and judgment. One such case, recorded in Acts, was his encounter with the Jewish magician named Bar-jesus. Being filled with the Holy Spirit, Paul looked the man straight in the eye and said: "You son of the Devil! You are the enemy of everything that is good" (Acts 13:10, TEV).

On numerous occasions Paul warned the Christian community concerning false teachers (Acts 20:29; 1 Tim. 1:3). In his debate with the Epicurean and Stoic teachers in Athens, Paul's gift of discernment was at its best as he delivered his Mars Hill address. These are but a few of the instances where Paul's superior perception is revealed.

Certainly the ability to discern reality is important to an effective leader. This capacity enables him to be decisive. He can be more accurate in his prediction of cause-and-effect relationships. Phony people are less likely to surprise him.

The Christian leader obviously has a plus in this area—the Holy Spirit. As reflected in Paul's magician encounter, the Holy Spirit was at work. Every Christian leader has access to this tremendous source of spiritual discernment.

*Spontaneity and directness.*—A spontaneous, natural style is another personal trait of a self-actualizer. Through this open, uninhibited, expressive manner, a self-actualized person comes across as real and human. He is not artificial.[9]

Words like *uninhibited, expressive, natural, direct,* and *simple* describe Paul well. He did not put on airs or mask his feelings. He made his feelings about John Mark's earlier behavior well known, as indicated in the passage beginning with Acts 15:36. In 1 Timothy 1:15, he calls himself the worst of sinners. After learning that the people in Lystra were about to make them gods, he and Barnabas tore their clothes and ran into the crowd shouting, "Why are you doing this? We ourselves are only human beings like you!" (Acts 14:15, TEV). On several occasions, Paul shook the dust off of his coat and feet when persons rejected his ministry and criticized Jesus (Acts 13:50-51; 18:6; 19:9). In Galatians 3:1 he is direct and stern in his rebuke concerning the Galatians' confusion about grace and law. Paul did not lack in directness.

Spontaneity and directness gives a leader credibility. This does not mean that a leader should not have tact. It does mean that he should speak the truth in love (Eph. 4:15). Persons soon lose their respect for leaders who vacillate and straddle the fence. It should also be noted that directness is not synonymous with being autocratic. A spontaneous, direct leader can be open and honest and allow others to have the same privileges.

*Courage in the face of opposition.*—A self-actualized leader is willing to stand up for what he believes. His superior sense of self-worth and adequacy allows him to take risks average persons avoid. His values are generally based on what is real to him rather than on what others tell him. Maslow stated that all the great creators he studied "testified to the element of courage needed in the lonely moment of creation, affirming something new (contradictory to the old)." [10] Self-actualizers are not only open to new ideas, but they are also willing to forego popularity in order to stand up for a new idea.[11]

Paul's courage is unquestionable. In Acts 21:13, he stated that he was ready to die for Christ's sake if necessary. Acts 14:19-20 recorded that after being stoned and revived by his friends he went back into the same city where he was arrested to preach again. An extreme and somewhat humorous example of Paul's boldness is his defense before the high priest Ananias in Jerusalem. After Paul had spoken, the high priest instructed those standing near him to hit him in the mouth because of what he had said. Paul's response was quick: "God will certainly strike you—you whitewashed wall!" (Acts 23:3, TEV).

Paul's courageous actions display a needed, but difficult, characteristic of leadership. A successful leader must develop the capacity to take risks and be prepared to stand alone against opposing forces.

*Confidence in self.*—A self-actualized person is a strong person. He has a low degree of self-conflict. His confidence and self-respect are based on the knowledge that he is a competent and adequate person. He knows who he is and, therefore, can give more energy to being productive.[12] A self-actualizer spends little time protecting himself from himself. Because of his superior self-confidence, he is also able to resist enculturation and maintain a certain inner detachment.[13]

Although Paul was honest about his war with his fleshly desires, he did not lack in self-confidence. He is quick to point out that his confidence stems from his relationship with Christ. Paul testified, "I have the strength to face all conditions by the power that Christ gives me" (Phil. 4:13, TEV). Again in 2 Timothy, Paul gave full credit for his self-confidence to God: "But I am still full of confidence, because I know whom I have trusted, and I am sure that he is able to keep safe until that Day what he has entrusted to me" (2 Tim. 1-12, TEV).

Self-confidence is not just a needed leadership characteristic, it is essential to effective leadership. A leader must feel the liberty to make his own decisions based on the knowledge that he is a person of competency and worth. Again, as in so many other areas, the Christian leader has available to him an extra portion: "The solid foundation that God has laid cannot be shaken" (2 Tim. 2:19, TEV).

*Positive attitude.*—Superior individuals, self-actualizers, do not dwell on the negative. Although they are not immune to fears and anxieties, they refuse to be pessimistic.[14]

Paul's positive attitude is clearly apparent in his letter to the Philippians. "Of course, my brothers, I really do not think that I have already won it; the one thing I do, however, is to forget what is behind me and do my best to reach what is ahead. So I run straight toward the goal in order to win the prize" (Phil. 3:13-14, TEV).

Many authors have attested to the importance of a leader's positive attitude. However, none say it more clearly and concisely than does Paul in this statement.

A leader who dwells on the negative will undermine the confidence of his followers. Eventually, his own feelings of adequacy will be shaken. A positive attitude does not imply a naive or head-in-the-sand approach. Certainly a leader must plan his work carefully. Good planning and decision making add to a leader's ability to be positive.

*A sense of limitless horizons.*—Maslow found that "a great number of self-actualizers have peak experiences, mystical experiences, the oceanic feeling, the sense of limitless horizons opening up to the vision." [15]

Paul exhibited this characteristic throughout his ministry. His Christian life began with his unusual conversion experience on the road to Damascus (Acts 9:1-9). Acts also contains the record of his vision regarding the Macedonian call (Acts 16:9), the vision of assurance in Corinth (Acts 18:9-11), and the vision of assurance concerning his safety in Jerusalem (Acts 22:17-21).

The most interesting example of Paul's vision, however, is different from the mystical experiences recorded in Acts. In his letter to the Romans he said that he had finished his work in Asia and was on his way to Spain (Rom. 15:22-24). What a vision! In Paul's day, Spain was considered the uttermost part of the earth.

Vision is the ability to see beyond the limits of one's immediate environment and time. The vision may come through a mystical experience, or it may be a part of a person's normal application of his God-given gifts. Great leaders have always been persons of great vision.

*Spiritual awareness.*—Maslow's studies also discovered that superior persons normally have a belief in a meaningful universe and a life which could be called spiritual. Nearly all have clear ideas of right and wrong. They believe in great ideals and values such as the transcendence of self; the fusion of the true, the good, and the beautiful; contribution to others; wisdom; honesty; the transcendence of selfish and personal motivations; and the giving up of lower desires in favor of higher ones.[16]

It goes without saying that Paul was a superior Christian person. His faith was the center of his life. All of his life and work revolved around his relationship to Jesus Christ. Paul referred to himself as "a servant of Christ Jesus and an apostle chosen and called by God to preach his Good News" (Rom. 1:1, TEV).

It is fitting to close this discussion of self-actualization and Paul's leadership by pointing to the importance of spiritual awareness. It is all too easy for Christian leaders to spend so much of their energies helping others grow that they forget to nourish their own spiritual life. Building and maintaining a dynamic devotional life is perhaps the most important area of growth for a Christian leader. No effort should be spared to pursue this challenge.

Paul should be on any list of superior persons. This great Christian leader of the first century is a model of effective leadership. As evidenced by scriptural references, his leadership bears out all of the superior traits that Maslow identified in modern-day leaders. Much can be learned from a study of his life and work. Although this chapter presents only a brief survey of Paul's leadership style, several lessons clearly emerge:

1. Be committed to a mission that you can verbalize.

2. Have a genuine love and concern for others.

3. Develop a support system of caring friends.

4. Pray that the Holy Spirit will improve your ability to perceive the real and the phony.

5. Be open, honest, and human.

6. Have the courage to risk and stand up for your convictions.

7. Be confident in the security of the Lord.

8. Approach your work with a positive attitude.

9. Under God, dream big dreams.
10. Make sure your spiritual base is sound.

## *Notes*

[1] Verses marked TLB are taken from *The Living Bible.* Copyright © Tyndale House Publishers, Wheaton, Illinois 1971. Used by permission. Subsequent quotations are marked TLB.

[2] From the *New American Standard Bible.* Copyright © The Lockman Foundation, 1960, 1962, 1963, 1971, 1972, 1973, 1975. Used by permission. Subsequent quotations are marked NASB.

[3] Frank Goble, *The Third Force* (New York: Pocket, 1971), p. 24.

[4] Ibid., p. 27.

[5] Colin Wilson, *New Pathways in Psychology: Maslow and the Post-Freudian Revolution* (New York: Mentor, 1974), p. 155.

[6] This quotation is from *The Bible in Today's English Version.* Old Testament: Copyright American Bible Society 1976. New Testament: Copyright © American Bible Society 1966, 1971, 1976. Used by permission. Subsequent quotations are marked (TEV).

[7] Wilson, p. 156.

[8] Goble, p. 26. (Chapter 2)

[9] Ibid., p. 28. (Chapter 2)

[10] Abraham Maslow, "The Need to Know and the Fear of Knowing," *The Journal of General Psychology,* 1965, p. 68.

[11] Goble, p. 28. (Chapter 2)

[12] Ibid., p. 29. (Chapter 2)

[13] Wilson, p. 155.

[14] Ibid., p. 157.

[15] Ibid.

[16] Goble, p. 31. (Chapter 2)

## *References*

Collins, Carl A., Jr. *Paul as a Leader.* New York: Exposition, 1955.

Goble, Frank. *The Third Force.* New York: Grossman, 1970.

Maslow, Carl A., Jr. *Motivation and Personality.* New York: Harper, 1954.

Wilson, Colin. *New Pathways in Psychology.* New York: Mentor, 1972.

# 6

# Barnabas: Hidden Leader
# of the New Testament

Robert D. Dale

Barnabas is the hidden leader of the early church. He is quietly tucked away in the pages of Acts 4, 9, and 11—15. Nicknamed the "Son of encouragement" (Acts 4:36, RSV), Barnabas was the first Christian on record to successfully bridge the gap between the Greek and the Jewish worlds. Born a Cypriote and reared a Levite, Barnabas linked the Hellenistic world and the Jerusalem church. He used his merged background both to separate clearly and yet to wed these two cultures. Barnabas, along with Paul, extended Christian missions to the Gentiles. In spite of this crucial contribution, Barnabas remains almost invisible among the leaders of the New Testament church.

A biographical study of Barnabas' leadership approach reveals a ladder-like structure. Each rung provides a stepping-stone for later ministries in leadership.

## Step 1: Barnabas Was a Leader Who Could Be Trusted

When the Jerusalem believers were pressured into dispersing because of governmental persecution, some unnamed disciples made a major evangelistic breakthrough in Antioch; they preached Christ to the Gentiles (Acts 11:19-21). The Jerusalem church had made Philip available to the Samaritans (Acts 8) and Peter to Cornelius (Acts 10). Now the Jerusalem believers deliberately sent Barnabas to do some evangelistic follow-up and new member orientation among the Antioch Christians (Acts 11:22-26).

Why Barnabas? Obviously, his background in the Gentile and Christian cultures gave him understanding and made him trustworthy to both groups. Additionally, Barnabas was the person "with the biggest heart in the church." [1] Later, the Antioch church would trust Barnabas to represent them in the great Jerusalem council described in Acts 15.

Trust is the human dynamic that is basic to all ministry. The ability to build and maintain relationships is fundamental to leading people. There is no evidence in the Bible's references to Barnabas that he approached the Antioch fellowship in anything other than a brother-to-brother relationship. Barnabas ministered as a peer, a fellow pilgrim in the way. Barnabas never hid behind a role. He wasn't Jerusalem's "religious inspector" to check out and straighten out the new Christians at Antioch. Barnabas knew that people trust persons, not roles. He knew that groups generally put more confidence in a helping brother than a bossy father.[2] Barnabas was trusted.

### Step 2: Barnabas Was Consistent in His Personal and Interpersonal Behavior

In his relationships with persons and groups, Barnabas was the same all the time. He was always credible and straight. Barnabas could be counted on to encourage and support others in their ministry. Like Andrew, who was always introducing folks to Jesus, Barnabas consistently offered encouragement to those who were trying to follow Jesus. "Son of encouragement" was an accurate name for friend Barnabas.

All of us need encouragement at times. Jess Lair in *I Ain't Well—But I Sure Am Better*[3] describes a good network of encouragers: a spouse who loves you, a job that challenges you, and five friends whose faces light up when they meet you. We need those shiny faces. They remind us of the persons in our lives who give us the benefit of the doubt, believe in us, and pray for us. Christians need that "cloud of witnesses" the larger fellowship of the church offers. But we need also an "inner circle" of friends to be a private church of support. No wonder Barnabas, the son of encouragement, was a welcome face as the Christian church began to expand.

### Step 3: Barnabas Encouraged and Supported Persons

Barnabas' spiritual gift was encouragement. First, Barnabas encouraged persons through his friendship. Paul was Barnabas' apprentice. If Stephen hadn't prayed as he died, Paul might never have preached; but if Barnabas hadn't forgiven Paul's past and sponsored him within the Jerusalem church, Paul would never have had the chance to preach in the Jerusalem fellowship.

John Mark is another example of Barnabas' supportive friendship. John Mark, a kinsman of Barnabas (Col. 4:10), joined Paul and Barnabas on the first missionary journey. However, he returned home to Jerusalem during the journey (Acts 13:13). When Paul proposed a second missionary journey (Acts 15:36), Barnabas agreed enthusiastically; but he insisted that Paul include John Mark in the missionary team again. Paul refused to invite the quitter. When Barnabas insisted that John Mark be given a second chance, he and Paul split up. Barnabas and John Mark joined forces and disappeared from the Acts account. Paul and Silas teamed up, and their missionary progress is the continuing saga of Acts. Barnabas believed in John Mark. Everyone needs a friend of that quality at points in his life.

Second, Barnabas encouraged others through his generosity. His first appearance in the biblical account is as an example of good stewardship (Acts 4:32-37). He sold his land and put all the proceeds into the church treasury. In contrast, Ananias and Sapphira only pretended to contribute generously, and were both stricken dead. In later years Barnabas would carry an offering from Antioch to Jerusalem to ease the plight of the famine-pressed Christians. A man not controlled by money, Barnabas encouraged others through his generosity.

Everybody needs encouragement. All human beings need some recognition. Or, as the transactional analysis theorists describe it, everyone needs "strokes." When a person doesn't get his strokes, his spine shrivels up and he dies. Without recognition a person becomes stroke deprived. And "stroke deprivation" leads to the "crazies." In other words, when people do not receive adequate recognition, they do strange things. They get irritated or angry or depressed or murderous or suicidal.[4] Barnabas stroked people. When people were around Barnabas, they felt better about themselves because Barnabas was constantly encouraging others.

### Step 4: Barnabas Could Balance the Task and Relationship Aspects of Leadership

As previously noted, Barnabas encouraged people; he was able to deal well with the relational side of a leader's role; but just as importantly, Barnabas could attend to task issues also.

Barnabas was missionary to the core. More than simply attentive to persons and concerned about their welfare, Barnabas was a worker who got the job done.

When he came [to Antioch]
    and saw the grace of God,
he was glad;
and he exhorted them all
    to remain faithful to the Lord
    with steadfast purpose;
for he was a good man,
    full of the Holy Spirit
    and of faith.
And a large company was added
    to the Lord (Acts 11:23-24, RSV).

Barnabas got results; his two missionary journeys indicate his concern for production.

A few years ago Robert Blake and Jane Mouton expressed a profound truth. An effective leader must integrate a concern for people and a concern for production. They picture this approach on a "managerial Grid." The ideal leader, according to the grid approach, is 9,9; he maximizes both his concern for people and his concern for production.[5]

*The Managerial Grid* ®

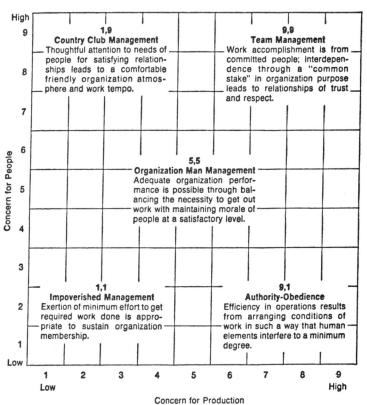

Barnabas had the 9,9 gift. His encouraging gift demonstrated his deep concern for persons. His missionary zeal indicated his commitment to production. Barnabas was a balanced leader.

## Step 5: Barnabas Could Select the Right Person to Get the Job Done

Barnabas did all he could to nurture the Antioch Christians personally. Soon, however, he discovered the limits of his own resources. What could he do then? Barnabas realized that he had to call in someone else who had more and different resources. He invited Paul to consult with him. Paul's superior training gave the Antioch fellowship access to new resources for Christian growth and development.

Barnabas evidently had a sixth sense regarding talent. He could see what Paul could become now that Paul's future was committed to Christ. An eye for talent in others is a key leadership trait. In a scene from *The Last Picture Show,* a middle-aged woman and a young man talk about Sam the Lion, a generous, compassionate, courageous man they both love. Sam had been the woman's once-in-a-lifetime love. She said, "You know, it's a shame to meet only one man in your life who knows what you are worth." [6] Barnabas could recognize a person's worth.

No ability is more critical to the effective ministry of leadership than the gift of selecting fellow workers. The most valuable resource in any church or volunteer organization is people. Reggie McDonough summarizes this truth: "An organization cannot rise above the quality of its leadership. The effective linking of the gifts and goals of individual Christians with the needs and missions of a church is absolutely essential to the success of the enterprise." [7]

## Step 6: Barnabas Could Equip Other People to Outgrow Himself

Love has been called "nature's psychotherapy." [8] Love can help us grow into someone we haven't been previously. Barnabas believed in others, and his faith freed them to grow.

Let's play a "what if" game. First, what if Barnabas hadn't guided Paul from a suspect outsider (Acts 9:26–30) to the leading missionary of the fledgling Christian movement? What if Paul had never been accepted into the Jerusalem and Antioch believer bands? Paul later wrote roughly one half of the New Testament. What if our New Testament was halved because no Barnabas vouched for Paul?

Second, Barnabas gave John Mark a second chance at missionary work. What if Barnabas hadn't stuck by his guns and insisted that John Mark be tried again? John Mark later wrote the earliest of the Synoptic Gospels. Not an eyewitness himself, Mark apparently wrote down the recollections of Simon Peter. No wonder Mark's account of Christ's ministry is so fast moving and vivid; Simon's impulsive nature and robust temperament are etched into every page. Wouldn't Christians today be missing a beautiful description of the words and works of Jesus if Mark had not set down the fast moving, "motion picture" Gospel?

Mark's Gospel also influenced the later Synoptic Gospels. For instance, Matthew uses 606 of Mark's 661 verses in his biography of Jesus. And Luke has 90 percent of Mark in it.[9] What if Mark had not been given another chance to outgrow his early mistake? Of course, God could have used other persons and means to develop a New Testament record; but isn't it a wonder to see the stewardship of Barnabas' life, although he apparently never wrote a biblical line himself in over half of the New Testament? What if? What if? Christians today can be certain that Paul and John Mark's contribution to the Christian faith was stimulated by Barnabas' ability to equip others to outgrow even Barnabas himself.

### Step 7: Barnabas Managed Conflict Constructively

When Barnabas and Paul disagreed over John Mark's place in the second missionary journey, they were direct in expressing their conflict. There was a "sharp contention" (Acts 15:39, RSV) between them. Rather than allow their disagreement to short-circuit the missionary enterprise, they looked for and discovered a "win/win solution." They created two missionary teams!

Barnabas and Paul apparently knew that conflict can be resolved in two destructive manners: win/lose and lose/lose. In a family-style community like the church, any losing resolution damages the climate and motivational level of the entire congregation. The win-win possibility was best for all. There's a forceful principle in this heated encounter between these two Christian giants: Disagreement won't damage Christian ministry if Christian leaders keep the redemptive purpose of God constantly in sight.

One footnote to Mark's story indicates the judgment of Barnabas. Paul writes to Timothy:

> Get Mark
> and bring him with you;
> for he is very useful in serving me
> (2 Tim. 4:11, RSV).

Other passages indicate that Paul and Mark worked together a full decade after their conflict (Col. 4:10; Philem. 1:24). This was indeed a constructive management of conflict!

### Step 8: Barnabas Was Flexible; He Could Either Lead or Follow

Barnabas discovered Paul; then Paul grew to be the leader. Barnabas never chafed or faltered; he could either be the spokesman or second the motion. Paul and Barnabas were a top-quality ministry team. "The person up front needs wise counsel from someone whose ultimate loyalty is at the feet of Jesus. Every Paul needs a Barnabas." [10]

Mrs. Sarah Ophelia Colley Cannon has learned the fine act of playing second fiddle. She set out in life to become an actress on Broadway; instead she became second best—a country comedienne called Minnie Pearl.

Minnie Pearl left her home at Grinder's Switch, Tennessee, for Ward-Belmont, an exclusive girl's school in Nashville. Then the depression hit, and Minnie had to quit school and begin producing plays as part of the WPA program. She traveled from rural town to rural town for six years. Country girls earned her most profound respect. Minnie identified with the dreams and disappointments of these plain girls. Slowly she developed a character and a backlog of stories. In 1938 in Aiken, South Carolina, Minnie Pearl was born as a character. Grand Ole Opry membership and financial success followed quickly.

Here's the conclusion of the matter in Mrs. Henry Cannon's own words:

> Success is not always
>     getting what you originally
>     thought you wanted.
> To me, successful people
>     are the ones
>     who leveled with themselves.
> They were able to realize
>     that in a lot of cases,
> second best is every bit
>     as good as first choice.
> We must realize
>     that many times
> our plan is not God's plan.[11]

Barnabas couldn't have said it better!

### Barnabas: a Good Man

Biblical names are often mirrors for the nature and temperament of the bearer of the name. Doctor Luke described Barnabas as "a good man" (Acts 11:24). George Truett, in a beautiful sermon on Barnabas, observed: "We cannot all be great men like Paul . . . . But we can be good men like Barnabas." [12]

Barnabas, a good man, was a good leader, too. He lived some leadership principles we can follow to effective Christian leadership. The following steps indicate the steps Barnabas used to advance the Christian message into a Gentile world.

8. Flexibility
7. Conflict Management
6. Equipper
5. Selectivity
4. Balance
3. Encouragement
2. Consistency
1. Trust

## Notes

[1] William Barclay, *The Acts of the Apostles* (Philadelphia: Westminster Press, 1957), p. 95.

[2] Taylor McConnell, *Group Leadership for Self-Realization* (New York: Petrocelli Books, 1975), pp. 19-32.

[3] Jess Lair, *I Ain't Well—But I Sure Am Better* (Garden City, New York: Doubleday and Company, 1975).

[4] Dorothy Jongeward, *Everybody Wins: Transactional Analysis Applied to Organizations* (Reading, Massachusetts: Addison-Wesley Publishing Co., 1973), pp. 65-66. Compare also, Claude M. Steiner, *Scripts People Live* (New York: Grove Press, 1974), pp. 44-45.

[5] The Managerial Grid figure from *The New Managerial Grid,* by Robert R. Blake and Jane Srygley Mouton. (Houston: Gulf Publishing Company, Copyright © 1978), p. 11. Reproduced by permission.

[6] Robert A. Raines, *To Kiss the Joy* (Waco, Texas: Word Books, 1973), pp. 133-34.

[7] Reginald M. McDonough, *Working with Volunteer Leaders in the Church* (Nashville: Broadman Press, 1976), p. 35.

[8] Eric Berne, *What Do You Say After You Say Hello?: the Psychology of Human Destiny* (New York: Grove Press, Inc., 1972), p. 88.
[9] Arnold B. Rhodes, *The Mighty Acts of God* (Richmond: John Knox Press, 1964), pp. 254-57.
[10] "How to Be Number Two," *Christian Leadership Letter,* a ministry of World Vision International, Monrovia, CA, edited by Ted. W. Engstrom and Edward R. Dayton, August 1977, p. 3.
[11] "Minnie Pearl's Success Road Rocky, Profitable," from *Amusement Week* in the *Nashville* (Tennessee) *Banner,* June 28, 1975, p. 4.
[12] George W. Truett, *We Would See Jesus* (New York: Fleming H. Revell Co., 1912), p. 90.

*Resources*

Alban Institute Materials. A complete catalogue of materials is available from the Rev. Loren B. Mead, The Alban Institute, Inc., Mount St. Alban, Washington, D. C. 20016.

Bennis, Warren. *The Unconscious Conspiracy.* New York: AMACOM, 1976.

*Christian Leadership Letter.* Individual copies available free from World Vision International, 919 West Huntington Drive, Monrovia, California 91016.

Engstrom, Ted W. *The Making of a Christian Leader.* Grand Rapids, Michigan: Zondervan, 1976.

Lassey, William R., ed. *Leadership and Social Change.* San Diego: University Associates, 1971.

Tagliere, Daniel A. *People, Power, and Organization.* New York: AMACOM, 1973.

Yokefellow Institute Newsletter. Subscriptions available from Lyle Schaller, 920 Earlham Drive, Richmond, Indiana 47374.

Leaders can be reminded through Simon Peter that neither Peter nor any other of the apostles was chosen for service because he was a finished product. A minister's call is a result of God's grace. It is a call based on his vision for what one can become, for what was within a person that could be touched by his power and shaped as he would have it. Recall the encounter of Peter in his call: "Jesus looked intently at Peter for a moment and then said, 'You are Simon, John's son—but you shall be called Peter, the rock!' " (John 1:42, TLB).

Peter in his humanness was himself, a learner. It was necessary for him to learn how to be what he was to be. Peter's learnings became the source of his actions. They became the basis of his behavior, the source of his model. He was shaped. His shaping becomes the basis of understanding of him as a profile for leadership. It was often with much struggle to hear and accept that Jesus taught Peter. Little by little the major elements of a leadership style appropriate for a leader in Christ's body, the church, became operative in Peter and visible through the Scriptures to leaders today.

The first element to emerge was faith. Specifically, the church must be founded on the unshakable foundation of a personal faith (Matt. 16:13-18). This confidence provided for Peter a release from fear of failure or defeat. It was to become the basis for bold action in the world in full assurance that this new community, gathered on the common ground of commitment to the lordship of Jesus, was unconquerable in pursuit of a mission of eternal consequences. Indeed what it "bound" or "loosed" on earth would be "bound" or "loosed" in heaven (Matt. 16:19). What it would do, would stand!

With Jesus himself as the "chief corner stone, elect, precious" and the promise that "he that believeth on him shall not be confounded" (1 Pet. 2:6), the Christian leader is established with confidence as he works. This knowledge that God himself is ensuring the victory makes it possible to work without unreasonable fear or wild excitement, which is frenzy. That the church will abide and accomplish its mission is promised to the "royal priesthood" (1 Pet. 2:6-10).

Through this faith, freedom is given the Christian leader to serve with confidence and peace. Discouragements will arise when sight is lost of this reality. Peter's fear became great panic when he lost sight of his Lord (Matt. 14:28-31). So will leaders today experience fear and uncertainty when they do not see the assurance of their efforts and faithfulness.

Effective ministry is continually dependent on such faith, whether it is expressed with bubbling enthusiasm or a more subdued calmness. "The toils and tribulations associated with this ministry, the sense of being misunderstood and the sense of one's own inadequacy, are enough to make faith unsure (cf. Lk. 22:32), to make love fail (cf. Jn. 21:17), to make the hope of overcoming the gates of death (cf. Mt. 16:18) seem faint. This ministry . . . is dependent every day afresh upon the grace of the Lord." [3]

The second element in the leadership style Peter

was to learn is forgiveness. If the Christian leader is to be effective in his leadership of the community of priests, he must himself be ready to express the character of his Lord. Peter learned from Jesus the radical nature of commitment required to live in and lead the new community of the church. To take the responsibility for reconciling action and to be always ready to offer pardon are necessary qualities for the leader (Matt. 18:15-22).

Who is there who has not been trespassed against by a brother? Who has not experienced the wounds of criticism, accusation, or offensive behavior in the effort to lead the church? And if the hurt comes, and comes again, pardon and grace will come with sufficient power—not in limited measure but in unlimited fullness. Peter provides the mirror for ministers' lives. Peter's own words as a Christian leader, after years of experience, reflect this quality of Christian leadership: "For this is thankworthy, if a man for conscience toward God endure grief, suffering wrongfully. For what glory is it, if, when ye be buffeted for your faults, ye shall take it patiently? but if, when ye do well, and suffer for it, ye take it patiently, this is acceptable with God. For even hereunto were ye called: because Christ also suffered for us, leaving us an example, that ye should follow his steps" (1 Pet. 2:19-21).

This does not so much call us to martyrdom as to modeling ourselves to the Spirit and behavior of Jesus. This denies the natural tendency to take the offensive by force of power and handle either people or situations. It is in the gracious expression of forgiveness that the criticism, the accusation, the offensive behavior is confronted at the deepest levels of human life. To come to conviction within that such behavior is unacceptable or wrong leads to conversion and submission to God.

Of equal importance as a dynamic dimension of the Christian leadership style was Peter's third instruction from Jesus. Peter discerned that leadership of the church was to be exercised with humility toward others. In the washing of the disciples' feet, Jesus taught Peter that leadership of the community was to take the form of servanthood (John 13:12-17). Peter had real problems with Jesus' action. He said to the Lord, "Thou shalt never wash my feet" (John 13:8). But Jesus responded by saying that until Peter had been served by Christ he had no part with Christ (John 13:8).

To be served by Christ gives ministers a part with him, and to have a part with him lays on them the pattern of his own behavior. This is far from the pattern that prevailed then and that prevails in the world today. Peter had to come to terms with the fact that leadership does not mean being served but serving. It means to be undergirding, not overlording—to be bent in service, not seated in splendor! Such a pattern is to be characteristic of the leader in the community of believers. All considerations of influence, prominence, power, or prestige are to be put aside in favor of the fulfillment of the leader-servant action by the Christian leader (Mark 10:35-45). The ministry must be executed as service to persons.

Peter's specific teachings on the role and behavior of the Christian leader reflect this understanding. To the elders and leaders of the church he said: "Neither as being lords over God's heritage, but being ensamples to the flock. Likewise, ye younger, submit yourselves unto the elder [older]. Yea, all of you be subject one to another, and be clothed with humility; for God resisteth the proud, and giveth grace to the humble. Humble yourselves therefore under the mighty hand of God, that he may exalt you in due time" (1 Pet. 5:3,5-6).

For the Christian leader, acceptance of the original idea of the primacy of service comes through the voluntary renunciation of power, but this is something that does not happen naturally. Hans Kung asks, "Why should any man, any authority or institution, give up something it possesses, and without any visible sign of something being given in return?" He answers this in saying, "The renunciation of power is in fact only possible for a man who has grasped something of the message of Jesus." [4]

Peter had heard and grasped that message, and he exhorted other Christians: "Neither as being lords over God's heritage, but being ensamples to the flock" (1 Pet. 5:3).

The final dynamic leadership element Peter received from Jesus relates to the motivation for service. "Feed my sheep!" Jesus said, not because you must or because you can or because you will, but because your love for me is expressed through this action (John 21:15-17). Peter, brought to Jesus by Andrew originally, had finally to discover his own internally validated basis for commitment to

Jesus. Love responding to love became the rationale for action for Peter. It also stands true for Christian leaders today (1 John 4:20-21), and Peter calls for ministers to respond to their call to express their ministry "not by constraint, but willingly; not for filthy lucre, but of a ready mind" (1 Pet. 5:2). How this call flies in the face of the idea of a forced surrender to an undesirable task or of being coaxed to extend ministry to the highest bidders. The call is clear: the Christian leader is a person who has experienced the love of God and his grace, who projects the outward expression of this love toward others not for gain or fame or influence but with a free and happy will.

Peter provides a positive model to help ministers become; but because he was human, he also provides a polemic profile. In three separate instances, Peter made mistakes that are common for the Christian leader. These mistakes are similar to tendencies ministers may follow today.

The first of these errors is that of confusing man's will and ways for God's. Leaders may assume knowledge and insight that exceeds that of others. This can include the knowledge of the Lord himself. Peter made this mistake in dealing with Jesus. Peter refused to hear his Lord when he announced the way of the cross as the means of the fulfillment of his mission. Peter took the position of knowing better than Jesus the way things should go. He took Jesus confidently aside and told him how he was to act and how things should happen. Hans Kung observed: "Peter, putting himself above his master, points out a way of triumphalism which will bypass the cross. Whenever Peter takes it for granted that he can think God's thoughts for him, whenever the confessing Peter of Matthew 16:16 becomes the misunderstanding Peter of Matthew 16:22, standing, perhaps without even noticing it, on the side of man rather than the side of God, then the Lord turns his back on him and delivers the hardest saying imaginable: 'Get behind me, Satan! You are a hinderance to me; for you are not on the side of God, but of men.' " [5]

Leaders are faced with the temptation to know too well and too much. Leaders may feel that the answers lie exclusively with them that their ways are *the* ways. If they make the mistake of asserting their will over others, they may assert their will even over God's and become what they should fear most, becoming the adversary of God.

The second leadership mistake Peter made was in being presumptuous about the strength of his own faith and the level of his own commitment. Confidently Peter declared that he would never fail or forsake his Lord (Matt. 26:35; Mark 14:31). Never would the call to service and faithfulness exceed his determination to be the Lord's man. But as Kung observed: "As soon as he self-confidently supposes that his loyalty is beyond question and that his faith is in a firm position, beyond any temptation; as soon as he forgets that he is dependent on the prayer of the Lord and needs to receive faith and devotion over and over again; as soon as he regards his strength and his readiness to accompany the Lord as his own achievement, as soon as in his self-confidence he overestimates himself and no longer puts his whole trust in the Lord, then the hour of the cock-crow is not far off." [6]

Finally, Peter gives us the polemic profile that comes in the mistake of imposing on others his own understanding of how God works and what he wishes for them. Just as Peter came to peace with the Lord about his own call, he concerned himself with another's call. As the Lord made clear that love called Peter to a special service and destiny, Peter began to measure others by the terms of that call. "What about him?" Peter asked (John 21:20-23). What's going to happen to John, the one who had always surpassed him in love? Kung observed: "Whenever Peter does not concern himself with his own task, whenever he tries to concern himself with everything, whenever he fails to see that there are things in human life that he cannot assume responsibility for, whenever he forgets that there are special relations with Jesus which do not have to pass through him, whenever he fails to accept that there are other ways apart from his way, then he will hear the word . . . 'What is that to you? Follow me.' " [7]

It is from these dynamic elements in the leadership style modeled by Peter that modern leaders may learn. In the positive dimension these elements include faith, forgiveness, humility, and service; in the polemic dimension, the mistakes of confusing one's will with God's, presumption about the degree of one's own strength and commitment, and the imposing of one's own understandings on others. All these add up to some considerable indicators of how to and how not to execute one's role as a leader in the church. Before a minister considers this at completion, however, he needs to look at the implications of these factors.

First, the Christian leader needs to have a consciousness that honors and recognizes the responsibility for the community rather than self. In today's culture, where the individual and individualism is the prevailing pattern, the idea of life in and through a community even at personal cost is a bit unusual; but the fact is that community consciousness rather than individualism is one feature of effective Christian leadership.

Second, the Christian leader must assume a position of humility rather than prominence. If prominence comes, it comes at the mighty hand of God who exalts. It must not come because the leader has engineered it himself.

Third, the Christian leader must renounce power as the basis of effective work. Except for the power of gracious love and congenial spirit, power is a violation to the structure and character of the kingdom of God. Not with power or might, but by my spirit!

Finally, four behaviors are called for:

*Evangelical humility.*—This involves the renunciation of titles that separate ministers from other believers. It also involves the elimination of the many barriers erected in light of supposed superiority of faith and Christian commitment.

*Evangelical simplicity.*—This involves the renunciation of special privileges, honors, gratuities, and considerations because one is a minister. Instead, a minister should adopt a life-style reflective of the values that honor kingdom values and not temporal splendor.

*Evangelical brotherliness.*—This involves the renunciation of alienation, separation, competition, and exclusiveness of ministers one with another or against other Christians. These things should be replaced by a spirit of collegiality with all other brothers and brethren.

*Evangelical freedom.*—This involves the democratization of the church through the liberation of the church's bondage imposed by ministerial autocrats. This requires an openness of spirit and the empowerment and enfranchisement of the lay members of the church.[8]

## Notes

[1] Hans Kung, *The Church* (Garden City, New York: Image, 1976), p. 604.
[2] William Sewell, "Getting to Know the Apostles," *Proclaim,* 7, No. 2 (1977), p. 12.
[3] Kung, p. 606.
[4] Ibid., p. 601.
[5] Ibid., p. 604.
[6] Ibid.
[7] Ibid., p. 605.
[8] Ibid., p. 607.

## Resources

Kung, Hans. *The Church.* Garden City, New York: Image Books, 1976.
Sewell, William. "Getting to Know the Apostles." *Proclaim,* 7, No. 2 (1977), 12-13.

# Additional Resources

**Leadership Bibliography**

Adams, Arthur Mennihew. *Effective Leadership for Today's Church.* Philadelphia: The Westminster Press, 1978.

Bass, Bernard M. *Leadership, Psychology, and Organizational Behavior.* New York: Harper and Row, Publishers, 1960.

Beal, George M. *Leadership and Dynamic Group Action.* Ames: Iowa State University Press, 1962.

Bellows, Roger Marion. *Creative Leadership.* Englewood Cliffs, N. J.: Prentice-Hall, 1959.

Cribben, J. J. *Effective Leadership Techniques.* New York: Macmillan Co., 1970.

Dobbins, Gaines S. *Learning to Lead.* Nashville: Broadman Press, 1968.

Douty, Mary Alice. *How to Work with Church Groups.* Nashville: Abingdon Press, 1957.

Drucker, Peter. *The Practice of Management.* New York: Harper and Row, Publishers, 1954.

Engstrom, Ted W. *Making of a Christian Leader.* Grand Rapids: Zondervan, 1976.

Ewing, David W. *Human Side of Planning.* New York: Macmillan Co., 1969.

Harris, S. L. *Leadership Unlimited.* Nashville: Convention Press, 1969.

Hillsdale College Faculty. *For Those Who Must Lead.* Chicago: Dartnell Institute of Business Research, 1966.

Howe, Reuel L. *The Miracle of Dialogue.* Greenwich, Conn.: Seabury Press, Inc., 1963.

Jennings, Eugene Emerson. *An Anatomy of Leadership.* New York: Harper and Row, Publishers, 1960.

Laffin, John. *Links of Leadership.* New York: Abelard, 1970.

Lippitt, Gordon L. *Leadership in Action.* Washington: NEA, 1961.

Phillips, Gerald M. *Communication and the Small Group.* Indianapolis: Bobbs-Merrill Co., Inc., 1966.

Rupert, A. *Leadership.* New York: McGraw-Hill Book Co., 1971.

Stogdill, Ralph Melvin. *Leader Behavior.* Columbus: Ohio State University Press, 1957.

Tannebaum, Robert. *Leadership and Organization.* New York: McGraw-Hill Book Co., 1961.

Tarcher, Martin. *Leadership and the Power of Ideas.* New York: Harper and Row, Publishers, 1966.